God
AND THE
Nations

God
AND THE
Nations

HARRY LACEY

JOHN RITCHIE LTD.
40 Beansburn, Kilmarnock, Scotland
GOSPEL FOLIO PRESS
P. O. Box 2041, Grand Rapids, MI 49501-2041

Co-published by Gospel Folio Press
P. O. Box 2041, Grand Rapids, MI 49501-2041
and John Ritchie Ltd.
40 Beansburn, Kilmarnock, Scotland

Gospel Folio Press ISBN 1-882701-56-9
John Ritchie Ltd. ISBN 0-946351-82-1

Cover design by J. B. Nicholson, Jr.

Printed in the United States of America

Contents

PART ONE

Foreword

This book is unique. We know of no other volume which, in such succinct form, brings before us the practical ways in which God manifests His sovereignty among the nations of the world.

Technically the sovereignty of God is not an attribute. Sovereignty is not something God *is*, but something He exercises. It describes His relationship to His creatures: He rules supreme over all. We may rightly say that before there were any creatures, when God dwelt in solitary grandeur, He did not have sovereignty—for there was no one over which to be sovereign.

This is a crucial point because it shows us that the sovereignty of God is controlled by His attributes. It is a fatal flaw in one's understanding of the ways of God to make His sovereignty His chief characteristic, making His true attributes subservient to His unrivaled authority in the universe. His love and holiness, His mercy and justice, and all other attributes of God determine the ways in which He exercises His control over human affairs. In short, what God *is* determines what He *does*.

The sovereignty of God is seen in Scripture, not as His right to act any way He wants—because no one can say no to Him, but by overruling the stupidity and stubborn-ness of men to bring them good, in spite of themselves.

This is seen most clearly in the Cross. The devil moved into Judas; Judas betrayed the Lord to the Jewish rulers; they handed Him over to Pilate; Roman soldiers executed Him—and the will of God was done!

We are not clever enough to understand all of God's dealings with the nations. We are not wise enough to read His love, mercy, and grace in every event recorded in our daily newspapers. God made one great declaration of His mercy and truth, His righteousness and love, at Calvary. Yet He does give us sufficient evidence in His Word and in our own lives that He knows what He is doing, that He is on schedule, and that in the end, when we see the whole scheme from the vantage-point of heaven, we will bow and worship the One who does all things well.

This book reminds us that God has done a considerably better job of getting the Word out than we may at first think. Will there indeed be someone in the heavenly choir *"out of* every *kindred, and tongue, and people, and nation"*? Revelation 5:9 says it is so. Evidently God *does* know what He is doing! We *can* rest in His love. The One who *"is not slack concerning His promise, as some men count slackness; but is longsuffering to us-ward, not will-ing that any should perish, but that all should come to repentance"* (2 Pet. 3:9) works on. Nothing will stop Him from accomplishing the purposes of His heart.

J. B. NICHOLSON, JR.
GRAND RAPIDS, MI.

Author's Preface

International intrigue, the subversion and fall of nations, the outbreak of wars, coupled with the fear of what may yet happen, during the past years have compelled men and women to ask whether God concerns Himself with the nations. Even those who think little on religious matters feel that God and the affairs of nations are in some way connected. Most have enquired if it is so. Some, in answer, suggest that He leaves them to work out their own affairs and does not in any way intervene. Others say that He may have taken a direct hand in the Old Testament days of visions and miracles, but that now in the Christian age He does not act in this way.

Does God silently govern above earth's din and war, and human and Satanic evil? Is He working a purpose in our day? If so, what is that purpose and what are His ways? Such questions matter a great deal, for the fortunes of nations, the issues of war, and the rise and fall of kingdoms affect us all. We can no more avoid the woes and throes of nations than life itself, for life and its circumstances are bound up with the life and circumstances of the nations in which we live.

These questions, and a hundred other relevant ones, have arisen and require answers. But where shall we turn for answers? If God Himself would speak, if He would explain, we would have certainty, and thus be able to think clearly in this confused world. But God *has* spoken, and His Word contains all things that pertain to life and godliness. Though He be a God who hides Himself (Isa. 45:15), He has revealed a great deal concerning the nations and His ways with them. Above all, His purposes are outlined on the pages of divine revelation.

The encouragement of this directed the writer to the study of the subject, and ministry on it was given during the winter of 1940-41. Believers in many towns and cities received such help that responsible brethren urged that it be written. At first the suggestion was not entertained because of consciousness of limited ability to carry it out, and lack of leisure in which to accomplish the task. But when the suggestion persisted from place to place, and was repeatedly voiced by different ones who knew nothing of the suggestions of others, the writer considered it an indication from the Lord which necessitated obedience. How much the author owes to others for help in the execution of the work it would be impossible to assess. Nevertheless it is possible for him to express his gratitude for all the help received in the compilation and criticism of the manuscript.

It is now sent forth in the hope that it may be made as much blessing in its written form as it has been orally.

H. Lacey
Cardiff, 1942

Preface to the Second Edition

This edition goes forth with deep gratitude to God that the first edition was so well received, and that this second one is both called for and possible in these times.

It is the desire of the writer that it may lead all who read it to a deeper realization of the greatness and goodness of *"the only God"* who, though *"invisible,"* is the *"incorruptible"* and *"eternal King,"* and that it may help to a better understanding of His ways in both providence and redemption.

The Christian reader is asked to give attention to the chapter, "The Church and Human Circumstances" and to the privilege and responsibility of the ministry explained there. It is the privilege of Christians to wait for God. They are not busy themselves in the efforts of men to construct a better world. Christ Jesus is their hope. It is theirs to keep the word of His patience and to allow their hearts to be directed by the Spirit into the love of God and the patience of Christ. Here indeed is the patience and faith of the saints. However, the writer is confident that, if this ministry were better and more fully discharged, many ills would be averted and temporal blessings procured for mankind, glory will be brought to God, and tranquil and quiet lives in all godliness and gravity made possible to believers. Not to speak of the reward afterward to those who will stir up themselves to lay hold on God in this way.

Some changes occur in this edition. These consist of one or two recast paragraphs and many typographical improvements. Most of these are due to the suggestions of Mr. W. E. Vine, who very kindly went through the first edition. Thanks are due to Mr. Vine and to all who have helped by making valuable suggestions.

The Ways of God

WILLIAM COWPER

God moves in a mysterious way
His wonders to perform;
He plants His footsteps in the sea,
And rides upon the storm.

Deep in unfathomable mines
Of never failing skill,
He treasures up His bright designs
And works His sovereign will.

Ye fearful saints, fresh courage take;
The clouds you so much dread
Are big with mercy, and shall break
In blessing on your head.

Judge not the Lord by feeble sense,
But trust Him for His grace;
Behind a frowning providence
He hides a smiling face.

His purposes will ripen fast,
Unfolding every hour:
The bud may have a bitter taste,
But sweet will be the flower.

Blind unbelief is sure to err,
And scan His work in vain;
God is His own interpreter,
And He will make it plain.

Part One

CHAPTER ONE

The Divine Warrant for the Study

The warrant for the study of the ways of God with nations is found in the stately language of Jeremiah 9:23-24, which holds a prohibition and an encouragement:

> *Let not the wise man glory in his wisdom, neither let the mighty man glory in his might, let not the rich man glory in his riches: but let him that glorieth, glory in this, that he understandeth and knoweth Me, that I am the Lord which exercise lovingkindness, judgment, and righteousness, in the earth: for in these things I delight, saith the Lord.*

We live in a day of boasters; arrogance and pride stalk the land. *"Men shall be boasters, proud, highminded,"* it is written. This kind of boasting and self-exaltation is surely unwarranted. Yet man is such that he must boast, must glory in something, must seek admiration, and if this escapes his attainment, how insignificant he becomes! The warning is that men should boast neither in what they know, what they can do, nor in what they acquire (though they are permitted to have these things).

Rather they are taught to have confidence in the knowledge of the Lord and understanding His ways in the earth.

Human wisdom is so imperfect, human might so feeble, and riches so fleeting, that it is folly to glory in such things. The short and narrow experience of men, their fractional knowledge, with their consequently limited ability to judge rightly, makes human wisdom puerile before the wisdom of God. He sees all with perfect vision in light which makes everything transparent, and, having exhaustive knowledge and eternity's experience as well as that of time, therefore decides accurately and always acts perfectly. The power of men, however great, when a fraction of His might is unleashed against it, becomes but a toy tossed in the tornado of the infinite. Riches, though massed mountain-high, are proverbial for their insecurity. The vast wealth of empires has passed and many a rich merchant has become poor in a night.

The folly of boasting in these things is evident. And though we use them, the heart is instructed to turn from them to something else in which to glory. Its wisdom will more than fill the mind, its might will more than awe the soul, and its riches will more than overwhelm the spirit. *"Let him that glorieth, glory in this,"* is the fiat of the throne. "Let him glory in that he knows My eternal being and supremacy and My ways in the earth." This knowledge of *Jehovah*-God, of His acts of lovingkindness, His works of judgment and ways of righteousness in the earth, is set before us for our understanding.

The 107th Psalm, which opens the last Book of Psalms, adds to the warrant for our study of the ways of

God by calling us to see how He regulates in turn the experiences of pilgrims, rebels, transgressors, and sailors. It shows that in His government God brings them into distressing circumstances in which—with none to help—they are brought to their wits' end, able only to cry to the Lord. No way of deliverance is open to them, no eye to see, no hand to help.

Then they cry unto the Lord in their trouble, and He bringeth them out of their distresses (v. 28).

He leads the pilgrim by the right way and brings the afflicted out of their darkness; He brings the sick from the gates of death, and makes the storm a calm for the mariner. Reviewing these ways of God, the Psalmist repeatedly bursts forth,

Oh that men would praise the Lord for His goodness, and for His wonderful works to the children of men!

The masterly summing up of the ways of God in the last eleven verses ends with the words, "

Whoso is wise, and will observe these things, even they shall understand the lovingkindness of the Lord.

So it is ours to observe these things, and to seek by the help of the Spirit to understand the lovingkindness of the Lord. Encouraged by this, let us turn to the law and to the testimony, applying ourselves to the Scriptures, which abound in evidence for our consideration.

As we search, questions will be answered, and we shall be surprised how much light is given on the ways of God with the nations, and how clearly He sets forth His principles and purposes. The Scriptures explain the origin of nations, and the apportioning of their lands, the secrets of the rise and fall of kingdoms and empires, and even the sad matter of civilian war and the deep mysteries of the morale of peoples. Kings and royal families, nobles and society, the men, women and children among the common people, are all spoken of in the oracles of God.

Having learned from the Scriptures the principles of God's ways, we shall be able to discern His hand in human affairs when we look around the world with its kings and governments, states and nations, cities and villages. As well, if we know the purposes of God, our estimate of happenings around us will be more accurate. Any tendency to question the ways of God will be turned to wonder, and our recognition of His wisdom will produce patience to wait His further working. And it will lift us in praise as we perceive mercy and lovingkindness woven throughout all His doings with the nations of men.

CHAPTER TWO

Three Spheres of the Works of God

It is essential for our present purpose to understand that the great works of God, so vast, diverse and intricate, belong to three distinct spheres: creation, providence, and redemption. It seems that much of what is found in the Scriptures may, with a little consideration, be apportioned to one or other of these spheres. From Genesis to Revelation we are confronted with the ideas of these three domains.

The *material* realm was created by God, who instituted and governs the ordinances of heaven and earth. In the realm of *providence* and moral government God, by means of circumstances, rules in an apparently indirect way, maintaining the great race of His creatures divided into nations, whose affairs He overrules in spite of sin and Satan. These two spheres constitute a platform for the greater sphere of *redemption*, eternal in its accomplishments, the message of which is proclaimed in the gospel.

The workings of the realm of providence and moral government will interest us most in these pages. The subject has difficulties and problems with which the godly of all ages have wrestled. So it must be recognized that, even if they could all be explained, they could not be dealt with in the scope of any human work. However, the fact of difficulties should not deter us from the consideration of the available evidence.

The address of the Apostle Paul at Mars' Hill (Acts 17:22-31) is one of the portions that introduce these circles of divine government which fill the rest of Scripture, summing up simply and clearly the ideas of each.

The God that made the world and all things therein, He, being Lord of heaven and earth, dwelleth not in temples made with hands, neither is He served by men's hands, as though He needed anything, seeing that He Himself giveth to all life and breath and all things.

This sweeping statement speaks of God as the Creator and Lord of the material realm and introduces us to the first sphere.

The sphere of our special interest is outlined in the second statement:

And He made of one every nation of men for to dwell on all the face of the earth, having determined their appointed seasons and the bounds of their habitation.

This introduces the moral realm, in which God is the Author of the nations, the Governor of their rise and fall, and the Lord of their destiny.

The realm of redemption's work, of which Christ is the

center, comes before us in the words of the third statement:

> *But now* [He] *commandeth all men everywhere to repent, because He hath appointed a day, in the which He will judge the world in righteousness by that Man whom He hath ordained; whereof He hath given assurance unto all men, in that He hath raised him from the dead. (*Acts 17:30-31)

This is the realm of the gospel, the spiritual and third sphere of operation of the works of God.

God who created and brought into existence these three spheres governs them all, *each one according to its own principles.* We are familiar with the laws of the material sphere—gravity, momentum, centrifugal force, the rotation of day and night, the sequence of the seasons—and we accommodate ourselves to them habitually, taking them as a matter of course. The success of the farmer and the gardener depends on their observing the laws of the seasons, and doing the right thing at the right time. The grim lessons of loss following disobedience to these laws, and the smile of the harvest following compliance with them, teach what Nature demands. Trial and error, success and failure, compose the experience that instructs men how to behave and fit in with the requirements of this realm of material things.

The second sphere of divine activities is no less a realm of principle: a sphere of different character in which we find principles of different character. In the realm of creation our actions are connected with things and processes, but in the realm of providence they are concerned with people and groups of people. The laws of creation govern behavior towards *things*; in a similar way the laws of providence and moral government are intended to regulate behavior, but behavior towards *persons.*

It is a familiar law that hot things will burn us if we touch them. Most of us, knowing this by painful experience, instinctively withdraw from the danger. If we disregard this well-known law, we suffer from its operation and reap the consequences.

Such a familiar instance of the working of Nature's law, known even to a child, serves to illustrate the working of moral laws in the sphere where our actions are with people rather than things. Wrong actions and unprincipled behavior will react, though not as swiftly, in the circumstances of those who disregard moral laws. This is God's world, not man's, and while men are, up to a point, able to choose their actions, they are not able to choose the *results* of those actions. The man or the nation that thinks it possible to cheat a moral God in a moral universe is a moral imbecile. The operation of this sphere of divine government leaves man helpless to avoid its consequences.

God may, however, by the introduction of principles of a higher order, defer, diminish, or, in some cases, appear to suspend those consequences. (See *Appendix* to this chapter.)

Not all the experiences of men are limited to dealing with things; nor do all the experiences of men end in dealing with people. There is a spiritual side to the experience of men, a phase of experience deeper, higher, more intense, more serious, and more far-reaching in its consequence. He is a wise man who learns how to behave in connection with things and processes of things, and a wiser man who learns how to behave morally with other individuals and groups of people. But he is a wiser man still who learns and observes the principles of the third realm, the realm of the gospel, where the hidden movings of the heart—its thoughts, desires, motives—are weighed, and if found to spring from other than love to God, are declared *sin*. For *"the law is spiritual,"* and demands that

> *Thou shalt love the Lord thy God with all thy heart, and with all thy soul, and with all thy strength, and with all thy mind, and thy neighbor as thyself.*

This goes a great deal farther than a person's action towards another. It goes so far as to require that action towards another shall be the fruit of adoring love to God. No wonder, viewed in this light, that the words are recorded, *"all have sinned."* This law, so searching and condemning, will be found to be as unbending as is the power of gravity and as impossible to remove. Refusal to believe that gravity exists will not alter either its existence, its working, or its consequences, nor will refusal to believe alter the existence, working, or consequences of the laws that govern sin in this spiritual sense.

When we discover the principles that govern things, we adjust our behavior in such a way that the laws bring to us their blessing rather than their curse. The farmer who has plowed early will be as thankful for the biting frost and the purifying snow as he will be for spring rains and summer sun. But should he plow in spring and sow in harvest, the law of winter will be a curse and the relentlessness of Nature will reward him with empty granaries.

The men of our day, as of every day, are not so foolish as to put themselves in conflict with things they cannot change. *"His God doth instruct him aright and doth teach him,"* says Isaiah 28:26. To those who will listen, God will teach a person the discretion that recognizes principle and submits to it, and in turn reaps its blessing and stores its good. So discretion in morals will also reap its blessing in circumstances. And, discretion, bowing to the laws that are spiritual, will result in the wisdom that will submit to the condemnation, *"all have sinned"* and will embrace the principle that, *"If we confess our sins* [to God], *He is faithful and just to remit sins, and to cleanse us from all unrighteousness."* The consequences of sin against God can be removed, not by an alteration of the laws and principles of this spiritual realm, but by the working out of them. The sinless and Holy One has suffered for sins, and because of this, those who acknowledge their guilt can be justified by faith in the Saviour and His sacrifice.

We have been introduced to the three spheres and have outlined a little of the ideas of each, but the object of these pages is rather to show what the realm of providence and moral government implies in the circumstances of men and nations. It has been necessary to define these spheres and to say a little about the character of these circles of divine activity and human responsibility. The necessity to compare and contrast these spheres and their principles will recur as we proceed in later chapters to discover what is revealed concerning God's ways with kings, governments, and nations, and observe the circumstances of rise and fall, prosperity and poverty, peace and war, from the origin of nations until the end of this age and the dawn of the Millennium. Then the nations of the earth will be ruled in full blessing and perfect righteousness by the Christ of Calvary.

APPENDIX: *The Problems of Moral Government*

Each sphere of divine government holds mysteries beyond the understanding of any human being. The questions that fill the concluding chapters of the book of Job (38–41) bring home to us a sense of how true this is in the physical world, the realm of things that are seen.

But the consideration of God's moral government is fraught with even greater difficulties. There often appears to be failure to execute justice on the wicked, and many evils seem to us to go unpunished. This problem has perplexed the godly in all ages: Job, Jeremiah, and the writers of Psalm 37 and Psalm 63 were at a loss to understand the prosperity of the wicked and the sufferings of the righteous.

Jeremiah, who was so intimate with God that he could expostulate with Him, asked once,

Wherefore doth the way of the wicked prosper; wherefore are all they at ease that deal treacherously? (Jer. 12:1).

At the time it appeared that the godly suffered and that the wicked prospered. But a few years told another story when the verses of Jeremiah 11:22-23 were fulfilled in the experience of the men of Anathoth, the very ones of whom the prophet complained. *"The year of their visitation"* came, and they were swept away in the Chaldean invasion that left their land desolate, while Jeremiah, in spite of suffering because of his service for the Lord, was preserved in the goodness of God.

The man of Psalm 73 evidently had an incorrect view of God's ways with the righteous and the wicked. Until he went into the sanctuary he exaggerated the apparent well-being of the wicked and seemed to take little account of the blessings of the godly. For a time he was obsessed with his own trials and by the fact that he did not then see the hand of God upon evil. But what he learned in the light of the sanctuary reassured him that there was no lapse in the execution of God's government. Eventually he confessed that the wicked do meet with retribution, however much it may appear otherwise. And the godly do find good here in spite of all their trials, not to speak of the immeasurable blessing of communion with God in their present experiences and of the joy of glory afterward.

The writer of Psalm 37 had become assured that, however otherwise it sometimes appeared, the unrighteous were cut down, even though at present they were seen to be in power, spreading themselves like great trees in their native soil (v. 35).

Job, during his trial, had a good deal of fault to find with God, but the end vindicated the righteous government of God. Not only did he receive twice as much as he possessed before, he emerged refined in character and enriched in the knowledge of God. Even his censorious friends had to come to him at God's direction so that Job might intercede for them (Job 42:7-10).

In view of the difficulties of these men, it is hardly to be expected that we shall be without ours. But whenever we have difficulties regarding any teaching of Scripture, it is well to remember the following:

—that the Scriptures present matters for faith rather than for reason;
—that we are unwise to allow what we do not understand to prevent our acceptance of what may be understood;
—that it is folly to reject a principle because in some cases we do not see its effect within days, months or even years. God does not run on our schedule;
—that it is by no means prudent to refuse fundamental rules because of seeming exceptions.

We will also take a look later at the problem of the sufferings of believers.

CHAPTER THREE

The Origin and Distribution of Nations

We shall discover the origin of nations by going back to the Book of Genesis, where we read:

And the sons of Noah, that went forth from the ark, were Shem, and Ham, and Japheth...and of them was the whole earth overspread (Gen. 9:18-19).

Chapter 10 provides us with three tables of names of families which spring from these three branches of the human race. Twelve families spring from the line of Japheth, about whom four statements are made:

...by these were the isles of the nations divided in their lands; every one after his tongue, after their families, in their nations (v. 5).

The line of Ham develops into twenty-six families, and about these the same statements are made:

These are the sons of Ham, after their families, after their tongues, in their lands and in their nations (v. 20).

From the line of Shem spring twenty families, of whom the same is said:

After their families, after their tongues, in their lands, after their nations (v. 31).

It seems that each family mentioned has its own tongue, is given its own land, and thus becomes a nation.

These are the families of the sons of Noah, after their generations, in their nations: and by these were the nations divided in the earth after the flood (v. 32).

In this interesting chapter we have the origin of the fifty-eight basic nations, to whose number God added later the nation of Israel miraculously developed from Abram (Gen. 12:1-3). As well, other nations developed later, such as the Moabites and the Ammonites from Lot (Gen. 19:37-38), the Ishmaelites (Ps. 83:6) from Ishmael (Gen. 21:18 and 25:12-18), and the Edomites (Gen. 36:43) from Esau (Gen. 36:1-43).

When Moses, the man with whom God spoke face to face, delivered his closing address to the nation of Israel, he confirmed the truth of the origin of nations by divine division when he said,

...the Most High gave to the nations their inheritance ...He separated the children of men, He set the bounds of the peoples according to the number of the children of Israel (Deut. 32:8).

The same truth is further confirmed by the words of God through the prophet Isaiah in chapter 44, verse 7:

I appointed the ancient people. So he writes:

*...God made of one blood **all nations** of men to dwell on the face of the earth.*

It is evidently the teaching of Scripture that racial distinctions and national barriers proceed from God who divides and departmentalizes the human race, rather than communizing it. The idea of one community of men, one family of human beings, is foreign to the Bible and contrary to the ways of God, both in providence and in redemption.

Since the second century after the Flood there have been nations, for during the days of Peleg the earth was divided (Gen. 10:25). His genealogy is given in Genesis 10:21-32, and shows that he was born 101 years after the Flood. This gives us not only the approximate time of the division of the human family but also the approximate date of the building of Babel, the symbol of human unity so signally confounded by divine intervention.

Furthermore, as we view the earth, learning something of its geography, marking the features of different continents, observing the zones of climate, the flowers and fruits belonging to certain lands, haunts of beasts found in one part that are unknown in another, homes of birds in some lands totally unfamiliar elsewhere, we have no difficulty in admitting that each land has a character all its own. Nor should there be any difficulty in going a little farther and admitting that it was so arranged by the hand of God. He made some lands mountainous, others not so; some with many lakes, some with few; some lands luxuriant, others less fertile. He is the author of the many characteristics that are peculiar to each land. Cold lands, temperate lands, torrid lands—all were arranged by the hand that spans the heavens and spreads the earth.

It is probable that earth was prepared thus with a view to separating the sons of men and moving the different families to as many different lands, that there each in its own inheritance might become a nation with its own individuality and live out its national experience before God.

The succession of terms, *"after their families, after their tongues, in their lands, in their nations,"* repeated three times in Genesis 10 suggests that it was the giving of a different tongue and a separate land to a family. Then as the family grew, it developed the people into a nation.

When the Most High divided to the nations their inheritance, when He separated the sons of men, He set the bounds of the people according to the number of the children of Israel (see Deut. 32:8). He *"determined...the bounds of their habitation"* (Acts 17:26).

God thus apportioned the inheritance of the nations: He moved the Japhetic group of families to the northern parts of the earth, the group of families springing from Ham to the southern continents, the Semitic peoples to the central belt; and later Israel received the crown of the lands in the center of all when God had developed that nation from Abraham.

Variety is always stamped on the works of God, and it may be fairly said that He never repeats Himself. All grass is grass, but there are hundreds of kinds of grass, and even within one kind not two blades are exactly alike.

All nature is evidence that God is the God of the individual. Monotony and uniformity do not mark His works.

Men are men wherever found, but every nation of men is different and, in fact, every man within a nation, though following the national type, varies from every other man of his nation.

The land where a nation dwells, the language the people speak, and the experiences of their history form national character and result in the people of one nation being different from the people of another nation.

People who live on broad fertile plains have a different character and outlook from people living among barren mountains or restricted valleys. The greatness and wealth of the fertile plain will mark the people who dwell there as the ruggedness of the mountains and restriction of the valleys have their effect on those who live among them.

Climate has its effect and compels habits that in turn form character. A language of richness and beauty will by its use maintain beauty of thought and richness of ideas and so contribute its measure of influence on the people who speak it.

Lands created by God, climate ordained by His hand, languages decreed by Him, and experience controlled by His hand developed different types and varieties of nations from the original families.

How wonderful are the ways of God! He first creates earth with its many regions, then from its dust makes man—the most wonderful of all His works—multiplies him to a race, afterwards dividing that race into many races, moving them each to its own appointed region with its particular character and climate, and there, speaking the languages that He has ordained, they fill the earth with their amazing variety.

From the natural point of view, it may seem desirable to unite mankind in federation, so working as one to accomplish human ambitions. But when men with complete faith in God follow the path of His will, federation is not necessary to human good. Individual dealing with God will itself produce a fellowship which is as superior to an arranged federation as a living human body is to a mechanical robot.

Both in the coming kingdom of God and in heaven itself, national distinctions seemingly will still exist (Rev. 5:9; 21:26). But it is declared in that day that *"they shall all know the Lord."* Though there will be variety among groups of men, and contrasting types suited to different positions, yet there will be peace. It will not be the peace of uniformity or monotonous sameness, but working in harmony, because every heart will be occupied with the same Lord and every life will be gladly surrendered to the same perfect control of love and wisdom.

The fact of different races and nations presents many problems today as it has done through the centuries. The problem of the Jewish race is a *"burdensome stone"* to the government of this and other nations. It has been suggested that the abolition of racial distinctions would solve the Jewish question. It has been argued, too, that wars arise because men are divided into nations. The suggestion is made that the fusion of nations into one commonwealth and the welding of races into one family would solve the problem of the Jew as well as the problem of war. If those things that separate, such as language, religion, customs, etc., were surmounted or removed, if men could become one, it has been thought that Utopia would result.

We live in a day when attempts are being made to unify mankind, and that these are but the forerunners of greater and more ambitious schemes is clearly revealed in the Word of God. It becomes evident to any with even a meager knowledge of prophecy that some success will accompany such attempts to unify men religiously, commercially, and politically, but it will be as anti-God in its object and prove as disastrous in its end as original Babel was.

The problem of the Jew and the bane of war will be discussed in later chapters, when we shall see that God has far different ways of removing these age-long obstacles and embarrassments of human society.

CHAPTER FOUR

The Times of Nations

Christians are familiar with that teaching of Scripture known as foreordination. Perhaps we had not expected to find such a principle working in regard to the nations. The remarkable verse that we have noticed before (Acts 17:26) contains three statements: God made the nations; God determined their times; and God appointed the bounds of their habitation. The second of these will interest us at this point—God determined the preappointed times. Or it might be paraphrased, God determined the arranged-and-being-arranged times of their rise and fall.

The rise and fall of nations had been decided by God in counsel long before the nations existed on earth. But just as the truth of Christian foreordination does not do away with human responsibility, so the truth of God's determination of the rise and fall of nations does not do away with national responsibility to God. Hence the peculiar tense of the word *"appointed"* or *"arranged,"* is *"pointed and being appointed,"* or *"arranged and being arranged."*

What a comfort to the godly in any day to know the rise and fall of kingdoms is governed by God! But lest we should take a fatalistic and irresponsible view, God guards His truth by this double sense of the word. The rise and fall of kingdoms is determined by God, and yet, whether we understand how it works or not, they are as well determined by religious and moral conduct of those kingdoms.

A clear instance of this appointing of times is found in the book of Jeremiah 46:17,

They did cry there, Pharaoh king of Egypt is but a noise, he hath passed the time appointed.

Judah had made alliance with Egypt to obtain the help of that kingdom against the threatened invasion of Nebuchadnezzar from the north; but Pharaoh's horses and chariots were of no help to Judah because the time of the fall of Egypt was come, and all its vaunted strength was but noise, crumbling to dust before the very monarch whom Judah feared.

Did we not see something like this in 1940, when it proved that the millions of France and all their military power were but a noise? France, too, had passed the appointed time. And as with Egypt of old, surely there were antecedent political, religious, and moral reasons. The fall of Judah and Egypt synchronized with God's delegation of power to Nebuchadnezzar, whom He made a king of kings and to whom He gave a kingdom, power, strength and glory. But when that same Nebuchadnezzar sinned against God in his pride, saying, *"Is not this great*

Babylon that I have built?" God brought him down, and he was made to know:

> *...that the Most High ruleth in the kingdom of men, and giveth it to whomsoever He will, and setteth up over it the basest of men* (Dan. 4:17).

Belshazzar, too, found that God had numbered his kingdom and finished it. He was slain on the night of his greatest sin, and Darius the Mede received the kingdom.

As far back as 1900 BC, Genesis 15 records a striking example of God's determining the rise and fall of kingdoms. God addresses Himself to Abram almost five hundred years before the occupation of Canaan by Israel, and says:

> *Know of a surety that thy seed shall be a stranger in a land that is not theirs, and shall serve them; and they shall afflict them four hundred years; and also that nation, whom they shall serve, will I judge...but in the fourth generation they shall come hither again: for the iniquity of the Amorites is not yet full.*

The fall of Egypt, who had enslaved Israel, synchronized with God's deliverance of Israel at the exodus, and the occupation of Canaan synchronized with the filled cup of Amorite iniquity. Egypt's behavior had merited divine judgment, and the Amorites iniquity was so great that they must be removed from before the face of God, whereas the affliction of Israel called for deliverance to a God of pity who delights in mercy even though He is a God of justice.

The prophets abound with so many instances of divine sovereignty governing the rise and fall of kingdoms that it would be impossible to quote a tenth of them. A list is presented in Jeremiah 25.[1]

Even the days of the power of the mighty Antichrist to come are limited and the appointed time of his fall is already set down in heaven. Though with Satanic aid and the world at his feet he thinks *"to change the appointed time,"* yet God has said:

Hitherto shalt thou come and no further, and there shall thy proud waves be stayed.

How this emphasizes the greatness of God and His sovereign wisdom! No wonder the Apostle Paul, as he viewed the ways of God, burst forth:

O the depths of the riches both of the wisdom and knowledge of God! How unsearchable are His judgments and His ways past finding out! For who hath known the mind of the Lord, or who hath been His counselor, or who hath first given to Him, and it shall be recompensed unto him again, for of Him and through Him and to Him are all things, to whom be glory for ever. Amen.

What a comfort to the godly in these days to know that God is still GOD in all His sovereign power!

...know therefore this day, and consider it in thine heart that the Lord He is God in heaven above, and upon the earth beneath.

How becoming, then, are the words:

Thou wilt keep him in perfect peace, whose mind is stayed on Thee: because he trusteth in Thee. Trust ye in the Lord for ever, for in the Lord Jehovah is everlasting strength!

ENDNOTE:

1 All the families of the north, the king of Babylon, Israel, Pharaoh, the king of Egypt, the mingled people, all the kings of the land of Uz, and all the kings of the land of the Philistines, Edom, and Moab and the children of Ammon, all the kings of Tyrus, and all the kings of Zidon, and the kings of the isles beyond the sea, Dedan, and Tema, and Buz, and all that are in the utmost corners, and all the kings of Arabia, and all the kings of the mingled people that dwell in the desert, all the kings of Elam, and all the kings of Zimri, and all the kings of the Medes, and all the kings of the north, far and near, one with another, and all the kingdoms of the world which are upon the face of the earth, are mentioned as being under the hand of God, who controls their rise and fall.

CHAPTER FIVE

The Government of Nations

The Scriptures teach that there are three distinct agencies operating in the government of nations. Human rulers with their various methods of government are well known; but this is not the only agency which directs the affairs of men. Two hidden agencies are at work. The Satanic system, composed of angels and demons, principalities and powers, headed by Satan himself, ceaselessly operates in innumerable ways to oppose the purposes of God, to seduce mankind, and frustrate human good. At the same time the great spiritual princes of God and His innumerable holy angels are sent to minister on account of those who are *"heirs of salvation"* (Heb. 1:14).

That human rule and the exercise of governmental authority are divinely instituted is evident from the New Testament passage:

> *There is no power but of God; the powers that be are ordained of God* (Rom. 13:1).

It is further termed *"the ordinance of God"* and the persons who administer it are described as *"the ministers of God."*[1] And the same teaching is presented in Daniel:

This matter is by the decree of the watchers, and the demand by the word of the holy ones: to the intent that the living may know that the Most High ruleth in the kingdom of men, and giveth it to whomsoever He will, and setteth up over it the basest of men.

The forms of human rule are portrayed in a vision given to Nebuchadnezzar and described in Daniel 2. A metal colossus in the figure of a man, with a head of gold, breast and arms of silver, belly and thighs of brass (or bronze), legs of iron, and feet of iron and clay, was presented in a vision to the king. In divine mercy the interpretation was given through Daniel, who explained that the gold set forth the rule of Nebuchadnezzar, a rule of absolute authority vested in one man.

This role would be perfect were it directed by a perfect being of infallible wisdom and infinite love. But though the form of rule, as the gold suggests, was best, it failed because the person in whom it was vested was by no means equal to his privilege and responsibility.

It was further explained that the succession of metals, which declined in value from the head to the feet, illustrated a succession of empires each with a different form of government. The silver breast and arms symbolized the empire which followed the Babylonian, and to which the Babylonian kingdom was given, as chapter five states (v. 28). It is described as inferior; and as it was inferior in neither wealth, power, people nor territory, it is concluded that the sense in which the inferiority is to be understood is in regard to the character of its rule.

A consideration of chapter 6 makes evident that this took the form of a limited monarchy, the laws of which were framed by the parliament of princes set up by Darius. Though they undoubtedly had the effect of limiting the power of the king to do evil, they also prevented Darius from acting justly toward the righteous Daniel.

The next form of rule illustrated by the thighs of brass was the Grecian (see Dan. 8:20-21), probably military in its character, whereas the iron presented the rule of a fourth world empire, which can only be Rome. That the rule of this power was so much stronger but so much less noble is well known.

Finally, the clay of the feet illustrated the introduction of an altogether new element in rule. The clay was interpreted as the seed of men and, obviously, the seed of men in rule. This indicates the voice of the masses, which limits the power of the iron of dominant rule, and results in the system presented by the toes, a federation of states, a league of nations. This league of nations form of human rule is clearly the one which will immediately precede the advent of Christ whose coming as the stone (see Dan. 2:34-35, 41-45) will remove all these forms of rule and result in the kingdom of God. Then absolute authority will be vested in the Lord Jesus Christ Himself.

Human rulers, whatever their character of rule, even though their power is delegated to them by God, usually follow their own plans to further their own ambitions. Even though at times they accomplish God's will, it is rarely intelligently done, nor is it because they desire to do so. In fact, they often act in contrast to His will when unknown to them Satan uses them for his base purposes.

In the fascinating twenty-eighth chapter of Ezekiel, there is a power behind a power, a king behind a king, a person more than human behind a person who is clearly human. In this mysterious chapter two monarchs of the rich merchant city of Tyre are portrayed. One is as distinctly human and earthly as the other is distinctly superhuman and belonging to another scene.

What strikes the reader of the chapter is that the character of the higher Being is stamped on the lower. The abilities and gifts of the greater are in measure imparted to the lesser, and because of these the human king becomes as illustrious in his realm as the great spiritual king is in his realm. What is more striking still is that the sins and pride of the greater are also seen in the lesser.

The same principle is presented to us at the end of the Book of God, for the Revelation pictures in the symbols of its thirteenth chapter an empire with its emperor crowned and reigning over many nations on earth. But behind this empire and its emperor is another empire and another emperor (portrayed in the previous chapter), none less than Satan and his angels, designated elsewhere principalities and powers (Eph. 6:11-13). He really exercises the power, governs the governor and rules the ruler. He really wears the crown. The amazing successes of some rulers and the uncanny prosperity of evil are attributable to this power over the powers.

But above all, and in spite of all, God sits sovereign, and by His wisdom, righteousness, and determination of purpose makes even what is violently opposed to Him to serve His purpose. He harnesses even the Devil's wildest and wickedest schemes to the chariot wheels of His unchangeable will as He goes on with His purpose in redemption.[2]

Occasionally God draws aside the veil which covers the unseen and we get a brief glimpse of the way in which heavenly beings have to do with the affairs of nations. Daniel 10:13, 20, 21, show that there were heavenly princes who, in the spiritual realm, stood for Israel. These verses also make it clear that there were evil princes standing in the same realm for Medo-Persia and Greece. They opposed the answer to Daniel's prayer which asked for good to be sent to captive Israelites.

Another glimpse is granted us in Zechariah's eighth vision, in the form of a symbolic representation of the spirits of the heavens. These four chariots with their horses of different colors probably illustrate spiritual powers who operate on mankind like the four winds of Daniel 7:2,. In this vision they are seen striving upon the sea producing the great states depicted there.

Evil agendas will not always be free to develop purposes of evil and hinder purposes of good. A day is promised when God will

...punish the host of the high ones that are on high and the kings of the earth upon the earth (Isa. 24:21).

Then Satan and his angels will be dethroned and bound (Rev. 12:7-9; 20:1-4), leaving only the unfallen angels and agencies of good to serve man (not to rule him). For then Christ and the new race of redeemed men will enjoy the place that God designed for man to have (Heb. 2:5-16). It is the purpose of God for man to reign, not to be reigned over; and although this has never been realized because of human sin and estrangement from God, it will be realized through the work of redemption. The redeemed, cleansed from their sin by the Saviour's blood and brought near to God, will, in communion with Him, delight in applying His will to earth.

At present, innumerable myriads of holy angels are directed by the hand that never errs and their work apportioned under the eye that never sleeps. These ministering spirits immediately fly at the bidding of the throne to do a thousand things[3] revealed and unrevealed in creation and providence, all of which constitute service for the sake of them that shall inherit salvation (Heb. 1:14).

As the two great spiritual agendas operate, the rulers upon earth, like great trees, are swayed by the winds of heaven, sometimes this way, sometimes that, sometimes wise and righteous counsels prevailing, sometimes evil counsels. But God goes on with His purposes, which will eventually ripen in the Second Advent of Christ, when the world to come will not be in subjection to angels, but be controlled by men in the glory, to which those men have been brought through the Kinsman-Redeemer (Heb. 2:14). Until that day, in spite of the chaos upon earth,

> ...the eyes of the Lord run to and fro throughout the whole earth to show Himself strong in the behalf of them whose heart is perfect toward Him (2 Chron. 16:9).

ENDNOTES:

1 The word used for ministers in Rom. 13:6, in comparison with other words translated servant or minister, is due consideration. It indicates service in an appointed office, and it will be seen from its use in the New Testament that a sense of sacredness is involved in its meaning. It occurs in the following passages only: Rom. 13:6, 15:16; Phil. 2:25; Heb. 1:7, 8:2.

2 God's supremacy as He rules in Providence over human rulers is expressed in three eloquent words:

> —He giveth it to WHOMSOEVER he wills (Dan. 4:25).
> —He turneth the king's heart WHITHERSOEVER he wills (Prov. 21:1).
> —He overrules so that they do WHATSOEVER His hand and counsel have fore-ordained (Acts 4:27-28).

3 The following list demonstrates the existence of the host of holy angels and suggests some of their activities:

> Genesis 28:12; 32:1-2;
> Psalms 34:7; 91:11; 103:20-21;
> Revelation 16:5, shows them in charge of departments of nature;
> Genesis 19:12-13, as executors of justice upon Sodom;
> 2 Kings 19:35, as executors of justice on Sennacherib;
> 1 Kings 19:7, they minister food to Elijah;
> 2 Kings 6:13-16, they protect Elisha;
> 2 Sam. 5:24, *"the marching of a military host"* aids David against the Philistines;
> Acts 12:5-10, they liberate Peter;
> Matthew 18:10, they care for children.

CHAPTER SIX

The Fact of Divine Visitation

Throughout the history of nations there have been times of disturbance, when peace has broken down and war has raged, when normal tranquility and security have been thrust aside and their place taken by stress and strain, hazard and danger. History records times without number when men have left peaceful pursuits for the violence of war, and when their constructive energies have been diverted into channels of destruction to the inevitable accompaniment of famine and want.

During these critical phases of human experience territories are violated, thrones upset, states broken up, cities wasted, homes wrecked, and the lives of men, women and children destroyed by the sword, famine, and disease. Such calamitous days have defied every effort of men to avert them. When present, they involve nation after nation and affect even those who do their utmost to avoid becoming embroiled. Because of the intrusion of these times, the history of man has proved to be a series of alternations between peace and war, and between circumstances of quiet and days of evil.

It was during one of these abnormal phases when a series of calamities befell a number of nations that Jeremiah prophesied. Habakkuk and Zephaniah were contemporary with him. The nations of the Middle East were convulsed in the throes of that trouble caused by the rise of Nebuchadnezzar. War and destruction had accompanied his coming to power; nation after nation was affected, until hardly a people in that area remained immune from the tribulation.

The days of the Assyrian monarchs who preceded Nebuchadnezzar were as much marked by these convulsions as the rise of the Persian, Grecian, and Roman powers in later times. Nor has the present era, the so-called Christian age, escaped, for through its centuries, in more or less severity, these phases have continued to alternate with times of peace, some shorter, some longer. This century has known some of the most fearful examples.

All efforts to eliminate these experiences have failed, and they continue to recur in the history of nations. Autocracy, oligarchy, democracy, social reform, education, religion have not been successful in their endeavors to prevent the outbreak of these nightmarish times.

Four thousand years or more of the history of nations have proved such crises to be unavoidable, though some would still not admit that they are unavoidable. But the fact is that no efforts to avoid them have succeeded, even though greater efforts than ever have been made. In spite of the spread of education, the development of culture, and the multiplication of the amenities of life, these times have recurred with even greater intensity and shorter intervals of peace than in ancient days. Though a League of Nations was formed, followed by the United Nations, disarmament instituted, and the world filled with peace schemes, every endeavor of the leading powers of earth to avoid these days has resulted in their increasingly becoming involved in convulsions which rock the whole world.

During the similar times of Jeremiah, to which reference has been made, it was asked,

Wherefore come these things upon me? (Jer. 13:22).

To this reasonable question a number of answers are forthcoming—from the political world, from the social world, from the religious world. The philosophers, statesmen, religious leaders, merchants and the common people all have their ideas.

In the minds of not a few, God is brought into the matter, and they put the same question in a different form:

Wherefore doeth the Lord our God all these things unto us? (Jer. 5:19).

Some think that these times are the result of processes—processes of moral government, a kind of reaping what has been sown. Others feel that, however true this is, there is as well something more direct than mere process and more personal than the inevitable rebound of men's policies and actions.

Many chapters of the Scripture are filled with the subject, and it may be said that whole books are largely devoted to elucidate the mysteries of such convulsions. In these it is shown that process has a good deal to do with their outbreak, but it is rather the burden of the prophets to emphasize that they are the result of intervention, which makes processes culminate in crises.

The Scriptures abound with evidences of the element of retributive justice operating normally in physical and moral life. But it seems that, even though these processes work, there are times when the evils of nations mount up in the passing of years and when the retribution of process accumulates and culminates in a storm which breaks upon whole nations. Such happenings were likened to a storm in Ezekiel 1:3-4, and Jeremiah 23:19.

In the conduct of the moral government of God, there are processes and there are crises; there is the normal and there is the abnormal. We find especially clearly in the Old Testament that God overruled to bring evil circumstances on groups of nations, circumstances not necessarily miraculously abnormal, but abnormal just the same. Examples can be seen in those which befell Judah and a dozen other nations in the days of Jeremiah and the group of prophets, Zephaniah, Habakkuk, Ezekiel and Daniel, who were his contemporaries.

To the direct question of the men of that day about the times in which they lived, there is a direct answer:

This is thy lot, the portion of thy measures from Me, saith the Lord; because thou hast forgotten Me, and trusted in falsehood (Jer. 13:25).

In a way unaccustomed to the average man, and a way

strange even to some professing Christians, the prophets attribute everything directly of God. Whatever part man might play or Satan might have, the matters with which the prophets deal are traced right up to the Throne, and attributed to the hand of God. This is presented in a remarkable way in a verse in Isaiah: *"I make peace, and create evil"* (45:7). It would be difficult to find a statement that bears on human circumstances more absolutely in its meaning than this one. For its simple words convey the fact that, whatever subordinate part man may play, peace comes essentially from the hand of God—*"I make peace."* In equally unmistakable clarity the statement concludes *"and create evil."*[1]

In the same absolute sense, whatever subordinate agencies operate, whatever part man plays, calamitous times proceed from the hand of God. And more, calamitous times are said to be not only allowed in a permissive way, but to be intentionally brought into existence, and in a direct way compelled among the affairs of men.[2]

Additional evidence of this is found in the record when Judah, in natural wisdom, had gone to Egypt for the military assistance of that strong power against the might of the Assyrian aggressor. In so doing they had not sought the help of God. In irony the Lord says,

> *Yet He also is wise, and will bring evil, and will not call back His words: but will arise against...the evildoers, and against the help of them that work iniquity* (Isa. 31:1).

In spite of all their efforts for help and protection, and

all their endeavor to avoid the evil, God in His wisdom and sovereign power

> *...shall stretch out His hand, both he that helpeth shall stumble and he that is helped shall fall.*

There is scarcely one of the prophets who does not in the same way directly attribute these times of calamity and fearful upheaval to the hand of God. The most striking of these passages are selected, and will be found on further enquiry to be supported by a host of others and to be backed by the spirit that breathes through the whole of the prophets.

Nine questions are found in Amos 3:3-8, all of which have an obviously negative answer. The first is, *"Shall two walk together except they are agreed?"* Obviously, no. The seventh one, which bears most directly of them all on the point of our subject, is really the climax of the argument of the prophet. Set out in this interrogative way, it is thus more eminently suited than a statement to compel the obvious answer. Its words are:

> *Shall evil befall a city and the Lord hath not done it?* (Amos 3:6).

In the same way as the other eight questions clearly require the answer No, so does this one. The truth conveyed therefore is inescapable: No! Evil cannot befall a city unless the Lord has acted. The force of these rhetorical questions seems therefore to require that all calamity is the direct result of divine action.

There may be a little nervousness in contemplating the

absolute sovereignty of God, whether operating in creation, moral government, or redemption, lest we should attribute evil to Him or seem to make Him responsible for wrong. But we shall find in further meditations that whatever actions He takes are necessary and form part of an ordered system of moral government. Though there are deep intricacies which none could hope to understand fully, much less to explain, yet revelations are made which we proceed to consider.

The ministry of Amos, which took place on the eve of calamities which befell at least eight nations, suggests the idea of a court. A significant expression recurs eight times, and in regard to each nation:

For three transgressions...and for four I will not turn away the punishment (Amos 1:3, 6, 9, 11, 13; 2:1, 4, 6)

This is otherwise translated, *"I will not revoke My sentence"* (DARBY). It appears from this that the guilt of these nations had been weighed, and the continuous evil, suggested by the expression *"for three transgressions,"* had called forth a sentence which awaited execution, but which might have been turned away had there been repentance. Instead, there was further sin, as is suggested by the term, *"and for four."* In view of this the waiting sentence must be executed for both the process and crisis of their guilt.

We find the same idea present in the ministry of the later group of prophets who stood before God on the eve of, and during the course of, the critical days of the rise of Nebuchadnezzar and the downfall of Judah. Zephaniah describes the Lord as a Judge who sits in the midst of the affairs of earth, a Judge who will not do iniquity, but will constantly bring His judgment to light (Zeph. 3:5).[3]

Of Belshazzar it is said that he had been weighed in the balances and found wanting, and that his kingdom had been numbered and brought to an end, being given to the Medes and Persians (Dan. 5:2-28). It is stated that the great Gentile monarch and his kingdom had been tried in a higher court than sits on earth and that, after investigation, their guilt had been proven. As the result of that, he was deemed unworthy to wield power any longer, and the kingdom to retain its previous privileges. Thus at the direction of that higher Court, the king was deposed and the people brought under the power of Darius, who received the kingdom contemporaneously with Cyrus in fulfillment of the prophecy of Isaiah 45.

In ways peculiar to each, all the prophets reveal the sovereignty of God operating over the affairs of nations. It is noteworthy that the book of Daniel, which has just been quoted, does so in connection with the empires of *"the times of the Gentiles"* (Lk. 21:24). These particular times began with the subjugation of Judah by Nebuchadnezzar and continue their unbroken course through all the centuries in which Jews are subject to Gentile powers. That this will hold good until the dawn of the millennial kingdom of Christ is evident from all prophetic teaching. It seems that at the commencement of these times light is given on Heaven's rule of these times. Scattered through the chapters of Daniel are fragments of evidence which, when collected and framed together, make a case that demonstrates that the rise and fall of kingdoms in times of convulsion is governed by God through the administration of the court of heaven and its angelic powers.[4]

Jeremiah, one of the few of whom it is said that he was chosen before his birth, was appointed of God *"a prophet unto the nations"* (Jer. 1:5, 10). Through him God revealed the same truth regarding the rise and fall of kingdoms, but with more detail. In his ministry it is shown that calamities befell a circle of nations because of God's controversy with them (Jer. 25:27-34). Visitation[5] is one of the prominent features of his prophecy. It is therefore, not to be wondered at that he is the prophet of tears. So close was his intimacy with God that he used it over and over again to expostulate with Him regarding the sufferings of the days in which he lived. In return God condescended to reason with the sincere and pathetic figure. As the feelings of man were expressed, so the pent-up feelings of a righteous God were explained (6:10-15), together with the necessity of dealing in visitation with Israel and the other nations.[6] It becomes evident from his ministry that while God dealt with Israel He also dealt with all other nations. Though it may be that the great light of that nation required more severe measures than were used upon others (25:29, 31, 32).

It is often said that God is not now in the Christian dispensation dealing with the nations. Within certain limits of meaning this statement is correct. As far as His redemption purposes are concerned, God is not dealing with the nations *as nations*. He is dealing with a world of *individuals* in gospel grace, calling out of the nations those who respond to the message, and incorporating them into the Church (this is more fully explained in the chapter on "The Purposes of God"). But while it is true that *as to His redemption purposes* God is not dealing with the nations, it is true that *as to His moral government* God deals with nations all along. Though His spiritual objects change in different eras, His government of the universe remains the same, and all its ordinances are servants to whatever purpose He has in mind in any age.

So with that moral government of nations and peoples—the rise and fall of kingdoms, the prosperity or adversity of nations, the woes and throes of war, or the tranquillity and calm of peace—all are governed by God now and serve the purpose of the spread of the gospel, the salvation of men, and the completion of the Church.

Throughout the New Testament there is evidence that the moral government of God operates at present. We find that a new realm with a spiritual object is introduced since the exaltation of Christ. But we find that it adds to the spheres which operated previously, not displacing them. When fully thought out, it will be seen that the conclusion that God has suspended His moral government is an impossible one; or that He has even replaced it completely by the introduction of a new realm.

Of course, the fact of a new realm, and the power of a new people can and should modify the happenings in the world (this is dealt with in the chapter on "The Church and Human Circumstances").

The Church is the prominent subject of the New

Testament. Nevertheless there is evidence of the working of moral government in regard to the Jewish nation, the ruling powers, the Roman world, and the people in general. Furthermore, evidence of the principles of moral government working in connection with churches and individual Christians is especially clear.

It is to be observed that many of the instances relate to individuals rather than to nations. Even so, that is not necessarily against the thesis of these pages. For the fact that at present this realm of government exists at all (unless there is clear evidence otherwise), requires that God still deals with states and nations in its operation.

That the Jewish nation is, in this age, under the hand of God is stated in the first Epistle to the Thessalonians. His wrath is come upon them and is evident in the circumstances of the nation as a whole, because *"they killed both the Lord Jesus and their own prophets,"* and obstructed the spread of the gospel (1 Thess. 2:15-16). They were warned of this in the words of the Lord (Lk. 13:1-6). Some of the people coming to Him told the Lord of the calamities caused by the collapse of the tower of Siloam, and by Pilate's brutality. These were warned not to construe these happenings to mean that those who actually perished were the greater sinners. They were instructed to observe them as tokens of like calamities which, on a greater scale, would fall on the nation as a visitation unless repentance was forthcoming.

The New Testament statement that, *"there is no power but of God; the powers that be are ordained of God"* (Rom. 13:1) conveys the same truth as the statements of

Daniel that *"the Most High ruleth in the kingdom of men and giveth it to whomsoever He will."* Whatever else it may convey, it seems to require the teaching that God now sets up and puts down kings.

An example of the execution of this is found in the life of Herod Agrippa I (Acts 12:20-23) in 44 AD. But the manner of its execution in this case is more miraculous than the usual operations of moral government.

That famine is one of the forms of divine visitation is shown in a later chapter. It is impossible to see how so widespread a famine as that which fulfilled the prophecy of Agabus and affected the whole Roman world could have taken place without divine decree. The nature and magnitude of it, as well as the fact that divine warning was given so that provision for the saints could be made, requires it to be a visitation (Acts 11:27-30).

When 2 Thessalonians was written, they, with the unbelieving world, were passing through tribulation described as a token of the righteous judgment of God (2 Thess. 1:5), evidently a token judgment that pointed to the apocalyptic judgments which will take place at the revelation of the Lord Jesus.

It seems that Peter, too, has present moral government in view when he spoke of a day of visitation (1 Pet. 2:12).

Moral government within the Church is the main subject of the fifth chapter of 1 Corinthians. It is the responsibility of the local Christian churches to act in judgment regarding those within the fellowship who offend in certain specified ways. Being gathered in the name of the Lord Jesus, the local church is empowered to excommunicate such offenders and thus deliver them over into a realm of things where Satan's power can inflict ill upon them. But while it is the responsibility of the church to act in this way toward believers, it does not need to do so in regard to the world. The simple reason: God deals with them by means of other agencies which operate under another economy. *"Them that are without, God judgeth"* (1 Cor. 5:12-13).[7] Obviously, *"them that are without"* the Church and its sphere of rule, God will deal with in His ways of moral government.

While Christians are inevitably affected by God's dealings with the nations in general (the Thessalonians suffered in the midst of a chastened world, 2 Thess. 1:5), they stand also in a place of still greater responsibility to God. For their behavior in the local assembly (1 Cor. 11:28-32) and their failure to judge themselves may result in God's dealing with them individually, according to higher standards than those with which He deals with the world. Bodily weakness, sickness, and physical death can come to Christians in the present as a judgment from God (1 Cor. 11:30-32). And churches can be dealt with judicially by Christ.[8] In light of this, Peter argues that if judgment operates pre-eminently in the house of God it must also affect the ungodly.

These passages taken together make a case for irresistible proof of the working of divine moral government in the present age. That this realm of government operates, that it has brought visitation on the Jewish nation, the Roman Empire as a state, and the general peoples of that empire, and as well, in a separate sense, has dealt with Christians and Christian churches (if there is no evidence of suspension or modification), requires the conclusion that God now acts in the same way.

Does it not follow, then, that the abnormal convulsions which have broken with irresistible force on the nations of the world in ways so similar to those recorded in Scripture are manifestations of the moral government of God? There has been no abrogation of the words, *"I create evil."* Nor does there seem to be any reason to suppose that the question of the Spirit through Amos, *"Shall evil befall a city, and the Lord hath not done it?"* can be answered in any other than a negative way.

Whatever part Satan and his hosts may play, or men or nations may have, the abnormal character and similar nature of these days seem to require that it is an overruling of Providence, and that it must be regarded as a visitation which moves along the same principles as those of ancient days.

But while we are compelled to this conclusion, we must beware of the error which Christ condemned, that of thinking that the individuals who suffer are the greatest sinners. Why certain individuals suffer must remain a mystery until God's day manifests the reason. But the fact remains that whoever suffers (and few can escape some form of hardship if not suffering) it is the nations with whom God deals. Regarding such dealings many revelations are made in the ministry of the prophets, some of whom have already been consulted. As we proceed they will need to be consulted again for further information.

Having now established the fact of divine action, it is

necessary to show from the Scriptures something of the *way* in which God acts. This the later chapters will do, each in its own way. The chapter on "The Forms of Divine Visitation" will show how these actions show themselves in human experience. The one on "The Sins of the Nations" will show the reason and cause why God should so deal with men. The one on "The Principles of Divine Visitation" will suggest some of the laws which seem to govern these outbreaks. The chapter on "The Objects of Divine Visitation" suggests the ends that are intended in these colossal and unspeakably solemn convulsions which men, by their natural wisdom or strength, are helpless to avoid, but which may be escaped by repentance toward God.

These visitations of abnormally evil circumstances, which make men cry out in pain, are to be contrasted with the great visitations at the end of the age. Then God will rise up to deal as never before with the world nations.

However severe the visitation past or present, it has never fully punished sin, nor completely restrained transgression, as Zephaniah confesses in 3:7-8. Men have hurried back to their evil ways again when there has been respite. But the great day of the Lord that is to come will fully deal with all forms of evil. These recurring wars seem to be tokens in a day of grace of the rising tide of divine wrath. Then in the apocalyptic visitations of the day of vengeance its full flood shall sweep earth clean of its sinners and its systems of evil.

ENDNOTES:

1 As used in Isaiah 45:7, *"I make peace and create evil."* Amos 3:6 states, *"...shall evil befall a city and the Lord hath not done it?"* Strong says, "This word evil is derived from a primitive root which means, to spoil."

It is not the word used normally as a noun for iniquity. While it can be used and is used in this sense, it is rather an adjective describing a condition, than a noun naming an absolute quality (though it is used as a noun). English translators have found it necessary to translate it by such words as affliction, adversity, harm, grievous, misery, grief, hurt, calamities, troubles, distress, sorrow, wretchedness, as well as by the word "evil" occurring in the quotations.

The following references which demonstrate the meaning of the term are only a fraction of what might be quoted to prove that it is evil in the sense of circumstance that is in view, and not, as some say, evil in the absolute. God did not and could not create evil in the sense of its absolute principle, though He does bring evil circumstances upon those men who follow Satan in the paths of lawlessness: *"evil from the north"* (Jer. 4:6); *"evil upon this people"* (6:19); *"evil upon them"* (11:11, 23); *"the day of evil"* (17:18); *"I will repent of the evil that I thought to do unto them"* (18:8).

2 It seems that the normal course of moral government, the abnormal times of visitation, and the miraculous interventions of judgment, all reveal that wrath of God to which reference is made in Romans 1:18. Bengel, Kelly, and many others have taken the terms *"tribulation and anguish"* (Rom. 2:9) to refer to the outworking of this wrath and indignation in the present, though obviously the climax of it is in the *"day"* of verses 5 and 16.

3 For a fuller exposition of this important chapter, see *The Process and Climax of Providence* in the section on the "End of the Age."

4 The following list gathers some of these fragments of evidence:

— *"the God of heaven has given the kingdom..."* (Dan. 2:37);

— *"a watcher and an holy one...cried...Hew down the tree"* (Dan. 4:13-14);

— *"This matter is by the decree of the watchers and the demand by the word of the holy ones"* (Dan. 4:17);

— *"this is the decree of the Most High, which is come upon my lord the king"* (Dan. 4:24);

— *"the Most High ruleth in the kingdom of men and giveth it to whomsoever He will"* (Dan. 4:25; so v. 17, 32);

— *"the heavens do rule"* (Dan. 4:26);

— *"God hath numbered thy kingdom"* (Dan. 5:26);

— *"thou art weighed..."* (Dan. 5:27);

— *"thy kingdom is divided and given"* (Dan. 5:28);

— *"the four winds of heaven"* (Dan. 7:2) symbolizing its unseen power, cause the convulsion which produces the empires, symbolized by the beasts;

— *"they said thus"* indicates that permission to destroy is granted from outside the empire (Dan. 7:5);

— *"dominion was given"* (Dan. 7:6);

— *"their dominion was taken away"* (Dan. 7:12);

— *"they shall be given into his hand"* (Dan. 7:25);

— *"there was given [Christ] a kingdom"* (Dan. 7:14).

5 The terms *"visit"* and *"visitation"* convey the idea of *"watching over"* and as a result of *"drawing near"* whether for the purpose of blessing or of punishment. Luke 19:44, referring to God's drawing near in the manifestation of Christ is an instance of its use in the sense of blessing. Inversely 1 Peter 2:12 shows its use in a sense of punishment. Throughout both Old and New Testaments both uses are found (compare Jer. 5:9 with 29:10), but in these pages it is used only in the latter sense.

6 The following passages will serve as an introduction to the evidence which Jeremiah's ministry provides:

— *"How shall I pardon thee?"* (Jer. 5:7);

— *"Shall I not visit for these thing"* (Jer. 5:9, 29; so 9:9);

— *"at the time that I visit them"* (Jer. 6:15);

— *"The year of their visitation"* (Jer. 11:23; so 48:44);

— *"This is...the portion of thy measure unto thee from Me"* (Jer. 13:25).

— *"I appoint four punishments"* (Jer. 15:3);

— *"I have taken away My peace"* (Jer. 16:5);

— *"I will cause to cease...mirth...gladness"* (Jer. 16:9);

— *"I will give thy substance, etc., to the spoil"* (Jer. 17:3);

— *"I will punish you according to the fruit of your doings"* (Jer. 21:14);

— *"I will bring evil upon them, even the year of their visitation"* (Jer. 23:12);

— *"l will send the sword, the famine, and the pestilence"* (Jer. 24:10);

— *"I will send...the families of the north...and the king of Babylon, My servant...against the land"* (Jer. 25:9);

— *"Like as I have brought all this great evil"* (Jer. 32:42); Jer. 5:22-29 and 25:29-33 will repay reading at length.

7 Some feel that there is a case for *will judge*, instead of *judgeth*. The Revised Version and the DARBY New Translation favor the latter. From the use of the latter word and the context, it seems that present moral government is in view.

8 Examples of Christ's judicial actions against churches or individuals include: *"I...will remove thy candlestick"* (Rev. 2:5); *"I...will fight against them"* (v. 16); *"I will kill her children with death and all the churches shall know"* (v. 23). It seems because the burden has to be held in the present that the purpose is to deal with the sin in the present.

The reward of faithfulness is assured by the moral government of God who, in the words of Christ, declares that an open door is set before the Philadelphians (see Rev. 3:8).

CHAPTER SEVEN

God's Witness to the Nations

God's governmental dealings with men are just. They are proportioned to the measure of their responsibility which, in turn, varies according to the measure of knowledge they possess. So to continue our enquiry we must ascertain the amount of light available to the nations. Then, after having proved the fact of divine visitation, we shall be able to appreciate its forms, principles, and objects.

The nations have never been without the light of divine witness, for each realm of God's government in its measure reveals the One who governs. Creation reveals His power; Providence shows His lovingkindness, judgment and righteousness; and Redemption makes manifest His heart of love. Man, in every state and every place, has at all times had divine light, though the way in which it has been communicated has varied, as well as the degree of light conveyed by each means.

Yet from the earliest days of man—before the inception of nations—God had His witnesses (Acts 14:15-17), unfolding the truth until the coming of the One who is the Truth. Steadily He gave more light until the true, perfect and ideal Light, which made known His grace and truth to His creatures shone through the incarnation of the Son of God.

The teaching of the Lord Jesus, contained in the New Testament Epistles and the Book of the Revelation, completes all revelation. Beyond this there is no new truth, no further light, though, of course, there should be progress in our apprehension of what has been revealed and is written for our learning. Sufficient has been recorded by the perfect wisdom of God to meet every need of His creatures, and it is evident from the principle contained in 1 Corinthians 4:6 that we are to be limited in our thinking to what is written.

The following means have been used by God to reveal Himself to men:

1. The witness of Creation
2. The traditional knowledge of God committed to Adam
3. The oracles of God given to Israel
4. The voice of circumstances governed in Providence
5. The incarnation of the Son of God
6. The New Testament Epistles and the Revelation

We shall briefly trace the development, use, and abuse of the earlier revelations of God and outline the later revelations that find their climax in the person of Christ.

The revelations of Creation, the traditional knowledge of God, and the voice of providence were made known to the nations from their origin. It is according to this that they are held responsible. The nations who in this age have heard the gospel have a much greater responsibility.

THE WITNESS OF CREATION

The universe is an abiding witness to the fact of God:

The invisible things of Him from the creation of the world are clearly seen, being understood by the things that are made, even His eternal power and Godhead (Rom. 1:20).

The vast firmament of the heavens, with its innumerable rolling orbs, the deep oceans with their unfathomed depths and untold mysteries, the vast continents with all their flora and fauna, and not the least, man in all the mystery of his physical and moral being, combine to present to us an object lesson of the eternal power and divine being of the One who has made them all.

No part of the realm of creation has yet been fully explored in spite of the great attempts of man, and it has to be confessed that man has no exhaustive knowledge of any part. Only infinite God could produce, maintain, and operate with such precision this wonderful display of measureless power and inexpressible beauty in which there is never a repetition in any species or kind.

Man's failure—in spite of all his knowledge—to comprehend the details of creation, and his failure—with all his inventive genius—to produce a blade of grass, demonstrate that creation sprang from the hand of a divine Being whose works are inscrutable and inimitable.

The hypothesis of evolution has been suggested to

explain the origin of species, without a word about the mind that designed them or the hand that governs them. Some have supposed that that which is too wonderful for mind to grasp, came into being without a mind, and that that which is unique and cannot be copied by human hand came into being without a hand. This illogical reasoning is not science. The hypothesis is confessedly unproved and apologized for by the statement that although undemonstrable, it is the best theory yet brought forward to account for our existence and that of the universe around us. Evolution, therefore, is not science, for science is demonstrable fact. It is only an hypothesis which masquerades as science, and so masquerading has become a servant of man's adversary to produce agnosticism and atheism.

Men would not insult one another by suggesting that they could believe that a watch came into existence without human mind and hands. Then how can they dare to insult their fellows by suggesting that they should believe all the world's grandeur exists and functions without the mind and power of a transcendently great Person?

All creation unites in one grand demonstration of His divine being and endless power, and its witness has been used from earliest days to bring home to the soul of the creature the truth of—GOD.

THE TRADITIONAL KNOWLEDGE OF GOD

(a) *Its Features:* The traditional knowledge of God, so called because it was handed down from Adam to succeeding generations, was composed of three features (possibly four)[1] and reveals more of the One whose power is demonstrated in creation. This knowledge showed in greater measure His character and presented the principles of His ways with man. The features were:

1. *The promise of a Deliverer* (Gen. 3:15): In the terms of a sentence on the serpent, God declared the coming of an Emancipator, a Saviour, who by crushing the serpent at cost to Himself would liberate man from the bondage into which his sin had brought him (for fulfillment of which see 1 John 3:8).

2. *The principle of blood sacrifice,* as the means by which the sinning creature may approach to God: This was exemplified in Abel (Gen. 4:3-6), continued through succeeding generations and was conspicuous in Noah (Gen. 8:20-22). It is suggested by Adam's coats of skins, derived as they were from slain animals.

3. *The presence of God on earth:* It seems by the language of Genesis 4:16 that the presence of God was known in a definite locality out of which Cain went to the locality of Nod. Genesis 3:24 states that God placed, or caused to dwell, the cherubim and the flame of a sword. It is most probable that the presence of God was known at the east of Eden in the same way as it was later known to dwell between the cherubim of the Mosaic Tabernacle and Solomon's Temple; the forms of these cherubim were probably the same as are described by Ezekiel in his first and tenth chapters.

(b) *Its Use:* The promise of a coming Deliverer, given

as it was at the time of the Fall, shows the mercy of God to the creatures who had sinned against Him and gave them the great hope of salvation from sin and Satan.

The sacrifice, instituted by God and accepted by Him, showed the principle by which that salvation should be realized and makes it clear that God desired His creature to draw near to Him. The fact that it was a blood sacrifice, in which a life is forfeited on behalf of the offerer, reveals a righteousness that can only forgive when justice is satisfied. The Presence amidst the fire and the cherubim demonstrated the holiness of God. From earliest days this light, supplementing the witness of the universe, was handed down from generation to generation until the days of Noah, when it became the light of those nations that were developed from the three branches of his family.

The nations at their inception were in the light of this truth and each commenced its separate national experience with a knowledge of the true God. This fact is stated in the treatise on the gospel written to the Romans:

> ...that which may be known of God is manifest in them; for God manifested it unto them. For the invisible things of Him since the creation of the world are clearly seen, being perceived through the things that are made, even His everlasting power and divinity; that they may be without excuse (Rom. 1:19-20).

It is evident that the early Gentile nations who lived without the later revelation of the Scriptures possessed as well the faculty of *conscience*, the indicator that, accusing or excusing, bears witness to right and wrong (Rom.

2:15). This inward voice of conscience, the outward witness of creation, and the communicated knowledge of God constituted the testimony of God to the nations and left them without excuse. Any darkness—spiritual, mental or moral—is the darkness of a perverted truth and rejected light.

(c) *Its Abuse:* It is recorded of the nations of antiquity:

…knowing God they glorified Him not as God, neither gave thanks; but became vain in their reasonings and their senseless heart was darkened. Professing themselves to be wise, they became fools, and changed the glory of the incorruptible God for the likeness of an image of corruptible man, and of birds, and fourfooted beasts, and creeping things (Rom. 1:21-23).

In these verses is traced the perversion of the nations from the knowledge of the true God to idolatry.

Man is a materialist and is never satisfied to walk before an unseen God as did Moses who *"endured as seeing Him who is invisible."* Moses walked by faith, but naturally man loves to walk by sight. It is this propensity that has continually led the nations into idolatry and drawn them away from the true God.

There is reason to believe that, in the third generation after the Flood, the great religio-empirical system of Nimrod represented the teachings of the traditional knowledge (probably on the plea of perpetuating the verbal promises) by material forms. This resulted in many of the nations, if not all, soon bowing to those forms as idols. The image of a woman with a child in her arms was used to represent the premise of the coming Deliverer—the woman's seed (Gen. 3:15). The altar of earth or unhewn stone, the simplicity of which gave the greater prominence to the sacrifice, was replaced by ornamented altars which were developed in beauty and ritual until the principle of life forfeited as an atonement was hidden in ceremony.

The stars themselves became objects of worship and the forms of the cherubim, lion, ox, man and eagle were represented by idols of similar form which were venerated and worshiped. In this way the channels by which truth was conveyed were worshiped as gods instead of God Himself. The ideas of the cherubim were perverted, the promise of a Deliverer and the principle of sacrifice degraded, so that they worshiped and served the creature rather than the creator (Rom. 1:25).

Thus the truth of God was debased into the lie of idolatry, and the pure morals of life lived in the wholesome fear of a holy and loving God exchanged for the degradations of unmentionable immorality and evil. In perfect justice God gave up the nations of antiquity, who thus had refused to have God in their knowledge (Rom. 1:28). Yet at the same time He caused the light of a new witness to shine in the midst of them by taking up Abram and developing out of his line the unique nation of Israel. In this way God raised up for Himself a witness which confirmed all previous witness and became a light to the succeeding generations of the world.

It is remarkable that the original forms of idolatry exist

in the world today and that many of their practices continue even in Christendom. These have been perpetuated by various branches of the original Chaldean priesthood instituted by Nimrod, represented today in every religion of the world as well as in certain social and commercial societies.[2]

THE ORACLES OF GOD TO ISRAEL

Wherein lies the superiority of the Jews? First of all, they were entrusted with the oracles of God. Having developed the nation and delivered them from Egypt, God revealed Himself to them at Sinai and committed to them the Law. At that time the nation was brought into covenant with God and under the curriculum of the tabernacle service.

In this way all that was revealed previously in the traditional knowledge of God, which had become so perverted among other nations, was confirmed and set down in permanent written form, the Ten Commandments in tables of stone, and the ceremonial law in the books we call Exodus, Leviticus, Numbers and Deuteronomy. To Israel belonged the line of prophets. By them God continued to reveal His mind and heart and to make known His purposes for Israel and the other nations. Conspicuous among all was the ever-widening stream of the promise of the coming Messiah and Deliverer and the ever-increasing revelations of the character and purposes of atoning sacrifice.

Jehovah made them His own filial race, gave them the

glory of His presence in their tabernacle and temple, made with them the covenants of Abraham, Isaac, Levi, Moses, Aaron, Phinehas and David, instituted the legislation of the Holy Moral Code, and the ritual with its divinely ordered symbolisms, and gave the promises of the "pleasant land." Last and greatest of all, out of them as concerning the flesh, Christ came (Rom. 9:3-5).

All these things made the nation unique and were unanswerable witness to God and His truth, the light of which spread far and near among the nations. This resulted in the proselytizing of many like the Queen of Sheba (1 Ki. 10:1-13), the Roman centurion (Mt. 8:5-13), and the Ethiopian (Acts 8:27-39). The Lord described them as the *"salt"* who were to prevent moral putrefaction and the *"light"* to show the way of God (Mt. 5:13-16).

THE VOICE OF PROVIDENCE

It will be seen in the following pages that the providences of God govern the circumstances of nations, generally causing hard times to follow evil practices and better conditions to be the fruit of righteousness, although grace often withholds the consequences of evil for a time.

These happenings are intended to be a voice to the nations and by means of these variations in circumstances God speaks more solemnly to men than by His words. These experiences operate on conscience, making men ask, almost in spite of themselves, what they have done to deserve calamity when it comes upon them. Later we shall see something more of the principles and objects of providence, so no more needs to be said here than that providence is one of God's witnesses to His creatures.

THE CHRIST AND THE LIGHT OF THE GOSPEL

In the Apocalypse the Lord Jesus is described as the Faithful Witness (Rev. 1:5), and John, in his Gospel, asserts that *"God whom no man hath seen at any time is declared by the Lord Jesus, the Only Begotten Son"* (Jn. 1:18). So perfectly does He express the Father and manifest the character of God, that when Philip said (Jn. 14:8-9), *"Show us the Father,"* the Lord Jesus replied, *"He that hath seen Me hath seen the Father."* Though God's power may be known by creation, His principles and holiness by the traditional knowledge of God, the voice of providence, and the Law of Israel, He Himself can only be known through a personal knowledge of the crucified and exalted Lord Jesus. This is the object of the incarnation, in which God was made known in human words and actions, and in which God dwelt with men in human form, expressing Himself in human experience. Of the Lord Jesus it was said, *"And they shall call His name Emmanuel; which, being interpreted, is God with us"* (Mt. 1:23). In His life and death every attribute of God was displayed and every grace of His heart shown out. *"He went about doing good,"* expresses His life, and *"He died for our sins,"* explains one of the primary reasons for His death.

After long ages of light (though incomplete and imperfect), the true and ideal Light shone forth—expected, anticipated and pointed to by each degree of earlier light. *"God, having of old time spoken unto the fathers in the prophets by divers portions and in divers manners, hath at the end of these days spoken unto us in His Son."* He is God's full revelation to man and God's final word to the world. When the preaching of the gospel is spoken of, it is said to be the preaching of Jesus Christ (Rom. 16:25) and *"the preaching of the cross"* (1 Cor. 1:18), which, after His resurrection and ascension, was heralded far and near by Spirit-filled apostles, prophets, evangelists and other Christians, and which has been told out in all the succeeding centuries of this age.

This message makes it possible for all who hear to come to a personal knowledge of the living Christ and Saviour and (through Him alone to) a personal knowledge of God. God's heart of love has reduced the terms of this blessing to the absolute minimum, for it is the nature of love to do all for its object. To believe the message and receive the gift is all that the individual needs to do. The word of inspiration is,

To as many as received Him, to them gave He the right to become children of God, even to them that believe on His name (Jn. 1:12).

Untold millions have received everlasting life and peace with God through the message, and many millions more blessed in environment and circumstances by the presence of Christians, which always results in moral and mental light.

THE LIGHT OF THE GOSPEL

A staggering verse confronts us in the first chapter of the letter to the Colossians, so staggering that many regard it as hyperbolic. Its twenty-third verse speaks of the glad tidings which were *"preached in all creation which is under heaven."* There may be hesitancy on the part of some to take the statement at its face value, allowing it to mean that the gospel spread through all creation within thirty years of the resurrection of the Lord Jesus. If this is the sense the Spirit of God would convey through the writer, then it follows that the darkness of heathenism is the darkness of a rejected gospel—either rejected at its presentation, after its acceptance, or lost from view in the course of years.

The commission to the apostles was *"to go into all the world and preach the gospel to the whole creation"* (Mk. 16:15), that *"repentance and remission of sins should be preached unto all the nations"* (Lk. 24:47; Mt. 28:19).

If due weight be given the facts, it will suggest that Colossians 1:23 is not as hyperbolic as it is sometimes thought to be. The miracle of Pentecost was a much greater one than most people realize. Acts 2 describes the occasion and tells us that there were dwelling at Jerusalem devout Jews from every nation under heaven. These heard the message of the gospel and about three thousand of them were converted and took a public place of testimony, being added to the company of disciples. Many, if not most, were strangers and probably returned to their distant homes, as did the proselyte from Ethiopia on a later occasion, bearing the message to tell to others in the power of their new-found joy.

It seems that after describing the first years of this age, the New Testament records largely the work of one man, Paul, saying little of the labors of the other apostles, evangelists, and untold thousands of Christians, all of whom were missionaries. It would surely require greater credulity to think that these were idle than to suppose that they obeyed the words of the commission and went to the nations with the message of the Crucified.

Fragments of history indicate hundreds of churches in North Africa during the second century and in Mongolia in later centuries, while from many other parts evidences of the spread of the gospel present themselves.

In view of the above, it seems necessary to admit a wide sense to the words of Paul, and to consider the darkness of heathenism to be in many cases the darkness of a rejected gospel.

The nations, whether at their origin, during their history in a past age, or their experience in the present age, have never been without light; and even when the light of higher truth has been perverted, the light of creation and the voice of providence continue to bear their testimony. So that at all times men are without excuse; and God, the Judge of men, is righteous in His judgments, whether it be His judgments executed in present circumstances or His judgment in the great day that is coming, *"when the secrets of men will be judged by Jesus Christ according to the gospel"* (Rom. 2:16).

ENDNOTES:

1 It is said of the stars, *"Let them be for signs and for seasons and for days and years"* (Gen. 1:14). Some have felt that God used these in early ages as a form of witness to the nations. The use of the star to guide the wise men from the East to Christ is suggestive (Mt. 2:2-10). But the subject is by no means clear. Even if they were used as a means of symbolically conveying truth, we who live in the full noonday sun of a completed revelation have no need to return to the details of the candle light of these signs.

It is significant that astrology has gripped most nations in much the same forms for many centuries, directing the heart to the worship of Satan and his host. Even Israel was given to the worship of the host of heaven (Acts 7:42).

If the stars served a divine purpose at any time, it is clear that through astrology they have been distorted for a Satanic purpose from probably Nimrod's days until today.

It may be that that which at one time was of God became debased into the astrology of ancient and modern paganism. If so the responsibility of the nations is the greater and their guilt the more severe.

2 See *The Two Babylons*, by R. Hislop.

CHAPTER EIGHT

The Sins of Nations

A group of prophets—Zephaniah, Habakkuk, Jeremiah, Ezekiel and Daniel—ministered during the fateful century which saw the end of Jewish monarchy and the beginning of the *"Times of the Gentiles."* During its years, through a great international convulsion, Judah's independence was lost, and the people were brought under the heel of the Chaldean despot. Daniel and Ezekiel, among others, were stripped of most of what they held dear, and carried away captive to the land of the successful aggressor. Jeremiah and others who were permitted to remain in the land suffered the miseries accompanying the servitude.

The calamities of that time, which had also reduced Tyre, humbled Egypt, and made vassals of all the surrounding nations, were likened to a whirlwind from the Lord (Jer. 23:19). Three waves of its fury visited Judah: the first resulted in the captivity in which Daniel and Ezekiel were carried away, the second reduced Judah to servitude, and the third left Jerusalem, the Temple and the land desolate, and the people scattered.

Between the captivity and the servitude, Ezekiel attained the age of accession to the priesthood. During his thirtieth year (which was the fifth of his captivity), the first of the visions which fitted him for his ministry was revealed. This is described in the opening chapter of his prophecy. From out of the north he saw a great whirlwind, cloud and fire; and out of the midst he discerned the forms of the sacred cherubim, and, accompanying them, great whirling wheels with rims full of eyes. At length his attention was directed upward toward the expanse from which he heard a voice, and to a throne, whereon sat a glorious Occupant in human form.

As he continued to look, his gaze was directed higher and higher, from being focused only on the storm—which symbolized the throes of the nations—until it took in the cherubim. These creatures pictured the agencies of Heaven, that, under the direction of the voice of the Sovereign, caused and controlled the storm.

In this way Heaven's control of earth's affairs was illustrated, and the great providences of God were explained. Beginning with the storm—at first glance seemingly uncontrollable—it concluded with a throne, the symbol of perfect control; opening with the dark cloud of forbidding judgment, it closed with the bow of mercy and faithfulness, the various colors of which, proceeding from the "Man in the Throne," suggested the blended attributes of the Sovereign, which shine out in all His ways.

Between these, Ezekiel had a glimpse of the Spirit-controlled cherubim, human in form, whose traits of character were suggested by the different heads. Also he discerned the great whirling wheels of divine government, and saw that at times they touched the earth, whereas at other times they were lifted up from the earth. Moreover, it was impressed on him that all obeyed the Voice, the hearing of which caused his attention to be drawn to the Throne. There he saw the One who uttered the commanding word, sitting in the place of supreme control.

What comfort must have been ministered to the perplexed exile! How it must have steadied his spirit to realize afresh that God was on the Throne! Still his Rock! Though kingdom and nation, ruler and crown, had crumbled to dust, yet in the unruffled calm of the peace outside of circumstances, the Monarch of uncreated heaven, and all created realms was still governing and working out His great purposes.

Nor was the vision of the sovereignty of God and the governments of Heaven the only one needed to fit him for his path of testimony and years of service. A further lesson was necessary—a vision of earth. But it was not a vision of earth from the aspect of earth, but a vision of earth from the aspect of heaven. This came to him eighteen months later as he sat in his house among some of the elders of Judah (Ezek. 8:1; 11:25).

The glorious Occupant of the Throne was again manifested, and He, by the Spirit, transported the prophet *in the visions of God"* to Jerusalem, the capital city of the nation which had suffered most of all the nations during those times of calamity (Ezek. 8:1-4). There, from a position between heaven and earth, were revealed the sins which resulted in the storm of visitation that caused the fall of the state and the tribulation of the people.

Whereas the first vision began with the storm on earth, and concluded with an unveiling of the Lord in the Throne, the second began with the Lord, and concluded with an exposure of the sins committed against Him. The direction of his gaze during the first vision was moved upward from the circumstances of earth until it was fixed on the Throne of heaven.

Subsequently the prophet was raised to the sphere of the throne and directed to look down. Prior to these experiences his ideas were inevitably limited, because they were in measure earthbound. But as the result of them, his perspective was adjusted to the throne, and his views of earth's happenings illuminated by the light of heaven. Had not the prophet been taken up in this way, his position among the people would have perverted his perspective, and natural bias and affection would have distorted his vision.

In the light which makes everything naked and opened (Heb. 4:13), secret sins were exposed, popular sins unmasked as serious crime, and religious practices which were supported by leaders were revealed to be blasphemous and impure. And in these was revealed the reason why the Occupant of the Throne, through the cherubim and their discerning movements, aroused a storm in the affairs of men and brought the whirlwind of Chaldean invasion out of the north.

Spiritual experience is similar in principle in every age, and its progress passes through much the same stages of development. The lessons in understanding the ways of God's moral government today follow the same lines as they did in Ezekiel's day. We first become conscious of sad visitations—circumstances like storm and wind and fire—in the affairs of the nations. Later it dawns upon us that the influence of another world is at work—the Spirit moves the cherubim and the wheels—and we realize that the heavens do rule in the kingdoms of men (Dan. 4:26). Furthermore, it is seen that the wheels are full of eyes, and we realize that the movements of Providence, so great and awe-inspiring, operate with perfect vision and discrimination in obedience to the Throne. Finally, the fact grips the heart that the Most High, acting through these agendas, rules among men.

Having been led through the progress of this revelation to a knowledge of the sovereignty of God, we may, from this viewpoint, look down, as did the prophet, on the affairs of earth. Only by this means shall we arrive at true values, and come to right ideas about the nations and the things which happen to them. Then things in which familiarity would prevent our seeing harm, things that popular opinion condones, things legalized by human laws, and even things gloried in as right, will take another form and adopt a darker hue.

No ecstatic vision may be ours, no mysterious revelation. The Word is open before us, complete, written for our learning, and from it we may receive all that is necessary to our understanding of the ways of God's government, and the why of His doings. As the written Word is perused it will be discovered that some of the sins which have resulted in visitation are political, others religious, whereas still others have a moral character. It will be in regard to these three groups that we shall consider something of what the Scriptures show concerning the sins of the nations. The lists that follow might be considerably lengthened, but space forbids little more than naming some of the more evident ones and quoting the passages that speak of them.

POLITICAL SINS OF NATIONS

(1) *A Broken Covenant:*

Shall he prosper? Shall he escape that doeth such things? Shall he break the covenant and yet escape?...Seeing he despised the oath by breaking the covenant...he shall not escape...As I live, surely Mine oath that he hath despised, and My covenant that he hath broken, even it will I recompence upon his own head (Ezek. 17:15, 18-19). (See also vv. 11-21.)

When Zedekiah broke the covenant with Nebuchadnezzar and despised the oath previously given, God spoke of it as sin, asking the question, *"Shall he prosper that doeth such things?"* answering it by the words, *"he shall not escape,"* and explaining the significance of Zedekiah's unfaithfulness in poetics as, *"Mine oath that he hath despised, and My covenant that he hath broken...His trespass that he hath trespassed against Me."* The form of the language in the question, *"Shall he prosper that doeth such things?"* suggests that a general principle is in view and seems to indicate that political treachery is trespass against God.

(2) *An Unprovoked Quarrel:*

I have not sinned against thee, but thou doest Me wrong to war against Me: the Lord the Judge be judge this day between the children of Israel and the children of Ammon (Jud. 11:27).

This twenty-seventh verse of this chapter presents the crux of the passage showing that Jehovah the JUDGE is judge of the motives of war. Unprovoked and unprincipled aggression resulted in the overruling of God which brought Ammon into defeat.

(3) *Unprincipled Means for Expansion:*

Thus saith the Lord: For three transgressions of the children of Ammon, and, for four, I will not turn away the punishment thereof; because they have ripped up the women with child of Gilead, that they might enlarge their border (Amos 1:13).

The prophet Amos, who explains the reason for the downfall of eight nations, tells us here that Ammon will suffer under the sentence of God for resorting to such means to enlarge their border. Instead of the enlargement they sought by evil means, captivity became the lot of the king and his princes.

(4) *Perpetration of Atrocities:*

Thus saith the Lord: For three transgressions of Damascus, and for four, I will not turn away the punishment thereof; because they have threshed Gilead with threshing instruments of iron (Amos 1:3).

Syria fell as a result of its merciless butchery of others. Its kings and nobles were broken and the people reduced to servitude.

(5) *Merciless Warfare:*

Thus saith the Lord: For three transgressions of Gaza, and for four, I will not turn away the punishment thereof; because they carried away captive the whole people to deliver them up to Edom (Amos 1:6).

The Philistines did not spare a remnant of their foes, their punishment directs that no remnant of them should be spared.

(6) *Independence of God and Confidence in Themselves, and their Handling of Nature and its Supplies:*

And the land of Egypt shall be desolate and waste; and they shall know that I am the Lord: because he hath said, The river is mine, and I have made it (Ezek. 29:9). (See also Isa. 19 and Ezek. 29.)

Egypt's fertile soil, watered from the river rather than directly by the rain, has been a snare to its people and will be again. For in their blindness they say, *"my river,"* and think themselves capable of control without recourse to God.

Such forgetfulness of Him and repudiation of His creatorial rights are followed by divine interference with the river, resulting in failure of fisheries, crops and manufacture, eventually causing the disintegration of the state.

(see the section on *Unemployment* in the chapter on "The Forms of Divine Visitation" for a fuller treatment of Isaiah 19).

(7) ***Pride in National Security:***

The pride of thine heart hath deceived thee, thou that dwellest in the clefts of the rock, whose habitation is high; that saith in his heart, Who shall bring me down to the ground? (Obad. 1:3).

Edom's folly in trusting to natural advantages, favorable circumstances, and fancied physical security is exposed by her fall under the visitation of God. "Unsinkable" ships have been sunk, "impregnable" fortresses have fallen: only in the fear of God is there safety for a nation.

(8) ***Antagonism to Israel:***

I will bless them that bless thee, and curse him that curseth thee: and in thee shall all families of the earth be blessed (Gen. 12:3). (See also Jer. 2:3.)

The principle that anti-semitism will be punished has not been abrogated. The parliament of princes set up by Darius deliberately framed a law against Daniel and his kind only to reap themselves the very evil they intended should fall upon the noble Jew. The scheming Haman of Esther's day proved that antagonism to the Jewish people was a boomerang, for it returned with awful force upon his own head. Ancient and modern history unite in proving examples of the permanence of this principle.

(9) ***Lack of Pity for a Fallen Nation—Rejoicing in its Fall and Joining in its Plunder:***

For thy violence against thy brother Jacob shame shall cover thee, and thou shalt be cut off for ever (Obad. 1:10) (See also vv. 11–14.)

Edom, believing itself secure, thought in its cruelty that it could plunder the fallen and go unpunished, but proved to its dismay that the Lord was Judge among the nations.

(10) ***Malignant Joy at the Fall of Another Nation:***

For thus saith the Lord God: Because thou hast clapped thine hands, and stamped with the feet, and rejoiced in heart with all the despite against the land of Israel; behold, therefore I will stretch out Mine hand upon thee, and will deliver thee for a spoil to the nations; and I will cut thee off from the people, and I will cause thee to perish out of the countries; I will destroy thee; and thou shalt know that I am the Lord (Ezek. 25:6-7).

Instead of being awed by the judgment of God upon another nation, and fearing the God whose hand had fallen so heavily, they gloated over the downfall of the smitten Israel. Surely they should have feared for their own sins, and have been silent before God, who had risen up to judge.

(11) ***Pride in Craftsmanship and Merchandise:***

Because thine heart is lifted up, and thou hast said, I

am a god, I sit in the seat of God, in the midst of the seas: yet thou art man, and not God, though thou set thine heart as the heart of God: behold, thou art wiser than Daniel; there is no secret that they can hide from thee: by thy wisdom and by thine understanding thou hast gotten thee riches, and hast gotten gold and silver into thy treasures: by thy great wisdom and by thy traffic hast thou increased thy riches, and thine heart is lifted up became of thy riches (Ezek. 28:2-5).

The cultivation of human genius and development of natural qualities for the self-aggrandizement of city and nation are followed by desolation rather than by glory, as the seventh verse of the same chapter indicates.

Behold therefore I will bring strangers upon thee, the terrible of the nations: and they shall draw their swords against the beauty of thy wisdom, and they shall defile thy brightness. (Ezek. 28:7)

(12) *Intrigue and Subversion of Other Nations:*

Because of the multitude of the whoredoms of the well-favored harlot, the mistress of witchcrafts, that selleth nations through her whoredoms, and families through her witchcrafts (Nahum 3:4).

Nineveh fell because of its lies and rapine and because through its witchcrafts and harlotry it sold other nations.

(13) *Failure to Acknowledge Divine Sovereignty:*

This matter is by the decree of the watchers, and the

demand by the word of the holy ones; to the intent that the living may know that the Most High ruleth in the kingdom of men, and giveth it to whomsoever He will, and setteth up over it the lowest of men (Dan. 4:17, RV).

Daniel 4:32 and many other portions prove that kings are set up by God. The fact that *"the powers that be are ordained of God"* (Rom. 13:1-2) puts a solemn responsibility upon every monarch of every land and every age. Pharaoh said, *"Who is the Lord that I should obey his voice?"* (Ex. 5:2), and boasted that he knew not the Lord. But the Lord whom he knew not taught him by circumstances that He, the Lord, was Sovereign. Nebuchadnezzar, Belshazzar, and Herod of the book of Acts, reaped visitations as the consequence of not giving God the glory.

RELIGIOUS SINS

(1) *Refusal to Hear the Message of God:*

But they refused to hearken, and pulled away the shoulder, and stopped their ears, that they should not hear. Yea, they made their hearts an adamant stone, lest they should hear the law, and the words which the Lord of hosts hath sent in his Spirit by the former prophets: therefore came a great wrath from the Lord of hosts (Zech. 7:11-12).

The sin of refusing to heed the message, stopping their ears so that they would not hear, was the reason why great wrath came upon these people.

(2) *Corruption of Truth Once Held in Sincerity:*

Thus saith the Lord: For three transgressions of Judah, and, for four, I will not turn away the punishment thereof; because they have rejected the law of the Lord, and have not kept His statutes, and their lies caused them to err, after the which their fathers have walked (Amos 2:4).

The law and commandments of God had become perverted by human additions and modifications. The people drew near with their lips, but were far off in their hearts, until such perversion and insincerity demanded that just judgment should not be turned away.

(3) *False Teaching:*

A wonderful and horrible thing is committed in the land; the prophets prophesy falsely, and the priests bear rule by their means; and My people love to have it so: and what will ye do in the end thereof? (Jer. 5:30-31).

God asks the solemn question, *"What will ye do in the end thereof?"* speaking of it as an *"appalling and horrible thing."* Religious corruption with the complicity of the people results in political decay.

(4) *Opposition to the Spread of the Gospel:*

Forbidding us to speak to the Gentiles that they might be saved; to fill up their sins alway: for the wrath is come upon them to the uttermost (1 Thess. 2:16).

When the ideas of men dominated teaching rather than the revelation of God, and when ceremonial details occupied the mind at the expense of the weightier matters of judgment, mercy and faith, as they did in the days of the Pharisees, they became the forerunners of woe followed by centuries of God's indignation.

(5) *Idolatry:*

For Solomon went after Ashtoreth the goddess of the Zidonians, and after Milcom the abomination of the Ammonites...And the Lord was angry with Solomon, because his heart was turned from the Lord, God of Israel, which had appeared unto him twice (1 Ki. 11:5, 9, RV). (See also vv. 4-10.)

Much of the Scriptures is devoted to the exposure of the folly of trusting idols and the sin of serving them. Man is still forbidden to make a graven image or any likeness of any form that is in the heaven, earth or sea, and still forbidden to bow to them or serve them.

Israel worshiped the calf that Aaron made, claiming it to be the material representation of God, who delivered them from Egypt (Ex. 32:4); but however plausible the profession of Aaron or the people, their sin involved rebellion against God (Ezek. 20:13), changing their glory (Ps. 106:19-21), and provoking God to jealousy by sacrificing to demons (Deut. 32:15-18).

Men are urged in the New Testament to flee from idolatry (1 Cor. 10:14) on the ground that what the idolaters sacrifice, they sacrifice to demons. It thus becomes evident that any offering or sacrifice to a material object, raised up in any name, even if it be the name of God or Christ, the saints or Mary, is a sacrifice to demons.[1]

(6) *Astrology; Witchcraft; Enchantments; Sorcery:*

Therefore now hear this, thou that art given to pleasures, that dwellest carelessly, that sayest in thine heart, I am, and none else beside me; I shall not sit as a widow, neither shall I know the loss of children: but these two things shall come to thee in a moment in one day, the loss of children and widowhood: they shall come upon thee in their perfection for the multitude of thy sorceries, and for the great abundance of thine enchantments. For thou hast trusted in thy wickedness; thou hast said, None seeth me; thy wisdom and thy knowledge, it hath perverted thee: and thou hast said in thine heart, I am, and there is none else beside me. Therefore shall evil come upon thee; thou shalt not know from whence it riseth: and mischief shall fall upon thee; thou shalt not be able to put it off: and desolation shall come upon thee suddenly, which thou shalt not know. Stand now with thine enchantments, and with the multitude of thy sorceries, wherein thou hast labored from thy youth; if so be thou shalt be able to profit, if so be thou mayest prevail. Thou art wearied in the multitude of thy counsels: let now the astrologers, the stargazers, the monthly prognosticators, stand up, and save thee from these things that shall come upon thee (Isa. 47:8-13). (See also Micah 5:12 and Nahum 3:4.)

These sins, so attractive to many because of their mys-

101

tery, their air of science, and their claims to unveil the unknown, were the direct cause of the fall of nations of old time. The spread of such things in our day is the forerunner of visitation.

(7) *The Worship of Nature:*

Who changed the truth of God for a lie, and worshipped and served the creature more than the Creator, who is blessed for ever. Amen (Rom. 1:25).

When the human being or any other of God's creatures is idealized, deified and served for its own sake (even if there is no image set up), it becomes idolatry in principle (sometimes leading to actual idolatry); thus, occupying the minds of the people with the creature, it displaces God and invites His displeasure.

(8) *Clairvoyance:*

Ezekiel 13:17-23 in part states:

Because with lies ye have made the heart of the righteous sad, whom I have not made sad; and strengthened the hands of the wicked, that he should not return from his wicked way, by promising him life: therefore ye shall see no more vanity, nor divine divinations: for I will deliver My people out of your hand: and ye shall know that I am the Lord (vv. 22-23).

The women condemned in this chapter seem to be like the modern clairvoyant, whose charlatanism and enslavement of the people is exposed and punished.

(9) *Spirit Practices:*

There shall not be found with thee any one that maketh his son or his daughter to pass through the fire, one that useth divination, one that practiceth augury, or an enchanter, or a sorcerer, or a charmer, or a consulter with a familiar spirit, or a wizard, or a necromancer (Deut. 18:10-11). (See also vv. 9-14.)

And when they shall say unto you, Seek unto them that have familiar spirits and unto the wizards, that chirp and mutter: should not a people seek unto their God? On behalf of the living should they seek unto the dead? (Isa. 8:19, RV).

Spiritism is stated to be the reason for the punishment of the nations of Canaan and the cause of the solemn commands to Israel to exterminate them. Seeking those that have familiar spirits, and through them, seeking unto the dead, is a precursor of hard times, hunger, fret, trouble, and anguish.

This list of religious sins may be expanded, but the main features have been presented in these references.

MORAL SINS

(1) **Unthankfulness to God for Creature Blessings:**

*Because that, knowing God, they glorified Him not as God, **neither gave thanks**; but became vain in their reasonings, and their senseless heart was darkened* (Rom. 1:21, RV).

This apparently simple sin of ingratitude is placed as one of the first steps on the downward road that ends in heathenism.

(2) *Ease, Idleness and Indulgence:*

Behold, this was the iniquity of thy sister Sodom; pride, fullness of bread, and prosperous ease was in her and in her daughters; neither did she strengthen the hand of the poor and needy. And they were haughty, and committed abomination before me: therefore I took them away as I saw good (Ezek. 16:49-50).

These were the sins that led to the downfall of the cities of the plain. Pride, fullness of bread and prosperous ease, instead of humility, restrained appetite and diligent labor, resulted in the haughtiness of spirit that persists in sin until it becomes abomination that calls for the intervention of God.

(3) *The Vanity of Women:*

Moreover the Lord said, Because the daughters of Zion are haughty, and walk with stretched forth necks and wanton eyes, walking and mincing as they go, and making a tinkling with their feet: therefore the Lord will smite with a scab the crown of the head of the daughters of Zion, and the Lord will lay bare their secret parts. In that day the Lord will take away the bravery of their anklets, and the cauls, and the crescents; the pendants, and the bracelets, and the mufflers; the headtires, and the ankle chains and the sash-

es, and the perfume boxes, and the amulets; the rings, and the nose jewels; the festival robes, and the mantles, and the shawls, and the satchels; the hand mirrors, and the fine linen, and the turbans, and the veils. And it shall come to pass, that instead of sweet spices there shall be rottenness; and instead of a girdle a rope; and instead of well-set hair baldness; and instead of a stomacher a girding of sackcloth; branding instead of beauty. Thy men shall fall by the sword, and thy mighty in the war (Isa. 3:16-25, RV).

The extreme development of feminine attractiveness by overdress, much jewellery and scents, coupled with artificial gait, and much use of the mirror, is denounced and visited, whereas the priceless feminine adornment of a meek and quiet spirit is praised in 1 Peter 3:4.

(4) *Lethargy and Indifference:*

Moab hath been at ease from his youth, and he hath settled on his lees, and hath not been emptied from vessel to vessel, neither hath he gone into captivity; therefore his taste remained in him and his scent is not changed (Jer. 48:11).

Moab's life of ease with unchanged natural taste and absence of discipline becomes the reason why they should be disturbed by visitation.

(5) *Avarice, Greed, Inhuman Treatment of the Poor:*

Thus saith the Lord: For three transgressions of Israel,

105

yea, for four, I will not turn away the punishment there-of; because they have sold the righteous for silver, and the needy for a pair of shoes: that pant after the dust of the earth on the head of the poor, and turn aside the way of the meek: and a man and his father will go unto the maid to profane My holy name; and they lay them-selves down beside every altar upon clothes taken in pledge, and in the house of their God they drink the wine as have been fined (Amos 2:6-8, RV).

This righteous sentence, that might have been turned away from the nation if they had repented, falls because of these sins.

(6) *Iniquity in Commerce and Unprincipled Trade:*

Such sins are involved in the previously mentioned reasons for Israel's fall and contributed to the fall of Tyre, Nineveh and Babylon.

(7) *Immorality:*

Mortify therefore your members which are upon the earth; fornication, uncleanness, passion, evil desire, and covetousness, which is idolatry (Col. 3:5). (See also Amos 2:7; 1 Thess. 4:3-7.)

Let no man deceive you with empty words: for because of these things cometh the wrath of God upon the chil-dren of disobedience (Eph. 5:6).

Lawlessness regarding marriage and the sanctity of sex, expressing itself in fornication, adultery and harlotry, is thus condemned.

The three preceding lists are made up of extracts from the actual experience of nations. Each fact is chosen by God for record in His Word. On every occasion it is evident that whether political, religious or moral, the sins are regarded as personally committed against God Himself.

These sins which, according to Romans 1:28-32 are worthy of death, are present in every nation; but it will be readily recognized that there is a great difference between the existence of these sins as an exception to the general behavior of a nation, and their existence as the rule of behavior. Sodom was not destroyed for the presence of these sins, but because of the predominance of them.

It is remarkable that in Daniel there are separate instances of the hand of God upon a king, a government, and a people. It has been observed already that this prophecy seems to suggest God's ways with empires during the centuries from the fall of Judah to their national restoration at the second advent of Christ.

Nebuchadnezzar abused the power entrusted to him personally, by his failure to give God the glory. He deified himself and commanded worship of the image. This pride further expressed itself in the fateful words, *"Is not this great Babylon which I have built?"* (Dan. 4:30), with the result that God humbled him by removing his reason. But though He did so, there is no evidence that the state or the people suffered. It seems that God dealt with him as an individual.

The later instance of the parliament of princes which Darius set up shows the hand of God upon a government. The wicked princes suffered the solemn consequences of their own laws, evilly devised against God and the godly, whereas Darius and his peoples were unaffected.

The fall of Belshazzar involved the subjugation of the peoples of the empire to the foreign despot; for the kingdom as well as the king was found wanting when weighed in the balances.

These instances of the hand of God are suggestive and seem to present the ideas that if kings sin as kings, God will visit them in that capacity; that if governments sin as governments, they will be dealt with as such; that if king, parliament, and people combine in iniquity, they will be dealt with together.

What is recorded of Syria in Amos 1:3-5 seems to support this idea. *"I will send a fire into the house of Hazael"*—the Syrian king (see 2 Ki. 8:7-15), *"which shall devour the palaces of Ben-hadad"*—the previous monarch. *"I will break also the nobles of Damascus"*— the leading society, *"and him that holdeth the scepter of the house of Edom"*—the royal family, *"and the people of Syria shall go into captivity"*—the rank and file of the nation.

Some think that, while these passages of Scripture record that which God has done, they are in no way pointers to that which He *does* do, nor in any way suggest explanation of that which He is doing. Nevertheless we cannot help feeling that all of these passages contain principles—principles of an abiding moral government, attested by the New Testament, and without the regulation of which the race could scarcely continue.

ENDNOTES:

1 There is a great spiritual system of demons, principalities and powers, headed by the Devil, which is collectively called *"rulers of the darkness of this world."* This system of spiritual wickedness uses man's necessity to worship, by all kinds of artifices, to lead nations into paths of religious activity which are rebellion against God. The success of this system in paganism is well known, but it is hardly less successful in Christendom's worship, perverted from the simplicity which is toward Christ.

The course of this world is said to be in accord with the *"prince of the power of the air, the spirit that worketh in the children of disobedience"* (Eph. 2:2). The Christian believer is delivered from this authority of darkness (Col. 1:13), and brought into the sphere of the rule of Christ, the Son of the Father's love.

The following quotation shows that visitations that have come upon nations for idolatry, have come in that form which exposes the utter foolishness of confidence in any but the living God. *"I will lay the dead carcasses of the children of Israel before their idols; and I will scatter your bones round about your altars"* (Ezek. 6:5), publicly showing that idols are no refuge in a day of calamity, being, in fact, themselves the cause of the calamity.

The following passages may be consulted: Ezek. 20; Jer. 10:1-16; Isa. 44:8-20 and 46:5-9.

CHAPTER NINE

Forms of Divine Visitation

It has been established that visitation manifests itself in the chastening circumstances which are created by God for nations. These circumstances do not take the same form. Storms, droughts, earthquakes, insect plagues, the ravages of beasts, unemployment, hard times, oppression, war, famine and pestilence, suggest the various characters in which visitation is expressed. Each of these may come in different measure of severity. The milder judgment of withheld blessing contrasts with the scourge of war or the infliction of famine. The character of the visitation seems to be related to the sins for which it is sent, and the measure of its severity to be proportioned to the degree of guilt. This will come out more clearly in the chapter on "The Principles of Divine Visitation."

Having considered some of the sins of nations, we now turn to a leading passage which will focus the mind on various forms of evil circumstances which from time to time have been the execution of divine decree.

The word of the Lord came again to me, saying, Son of

man, when the land sinneth against Me by committing a trespass, and I stretch out Mine hand upon it, and break the staff of the bread thereof, and send famine upon it, and cut off from it man and beast; though these three men, Noah, Daniel and Job, were in it they should deliver but their own souls by their righteousness, saith the Lord God. If I cause noisome beasts to pass through the land, and they spoil it, so that it be desolate, that no man may pass through because of the beasts; though these three men were in it, as I live, saith the Lord God, they shall deliver neither sons nor daughters; they only shall be delivered, but the land shall be desolate. Or if I bring a sword upon that land, and say, Sword, go through the land; so that I cut off from it man and beast; though these three men were in it, as I live, saith the Lord God, they shall deliver neither sons nor daughters, but they only shall be delivered themselves. Or if I send a pestilence into that land, and pour out My fury upon it in blood, to cut off from it man and beast: though Noah, Daniel and Job were in it, as I live, saith the Lord God, they shall deliver neither son nor daughter; they shall but deliver their own souls by their righteousness. For thus saith the Lord God; How much more when I send My four sore judgments upon Jerusalem, the sword, and the famine, and the noisome beasts, and the pestilence, to cut off from it man and beast? (Ezek. 14:12-21).

This passage mentions four forms of divine visitation: famine, evil beasts, sword and pestilence, which are applicable to any and every land; it argues that if God deals thus with other lands, He will also deal with Jerusalem in the same ways.

These instruments which God uses as voices to nations are supplemented in the following list, which contains statements of other kinds of visitation. The relevant passages are quoted in each case, and in most cases examples are given.

(1) *Drought causing Barrenness and Famine:*

He turneth rivers into a wilderness, and watersprings into a thirsty ground: a fruitful land into a salt desert, for the wickedness of them that dwell therein (Ps. 107:33-34). (See also Jer. 3:3.)

In the time of their visitation they shall be cast down, saith the Lord. I will utterly consume them, saith the Lord: there shall be no grapes on the vine, nor figs on the fig tree, and the leaf shall fade; and the things that I have given them shall pass away from them (Jer. 8:12-13).

Elisha's words to the Shunammite (2 Ki. 8:1), *"The Lord hath called for a famine,"* is one of the many Old Testament instances of the working out of this. Its parallel in New Testament days is found in Acts 11:28, where the prophet Agabus foretold the great dearth that was to afflict the world of the Roman Empire in the days of Claudius Caesar. It seems significant that, after promise of better conduct than some of his predecessors, Claudius Caesar sank to a degradation worse than many of them.

113

(2) *Storms:*

Hast thou entered into the treasures of the snow? or hast thou seen the treasures of the hail, which I have reserved against the time of trouble, against the day of battle and war? (Job 38:22-23).

Thou shalt be visited of the Lord of hosts with thunder, and with earthquake, and great noise, with whirlwind and tempest, and the flame of a devouring fire (Isa. 29:6).

And I will plead against him with pestilence and with blood; and I will rain upon him, and upon his hordes, and upon the many peoples that are with him, an overflowing shower, and great hailstorms, fire, and brimstone (Ezek. 38:22).

He gave up their cattle also to the hail, and their flocks to hot thunderbolts (Ps. 78:48). (See also Ps. 48:7.)

The story of Jonah furnishes an instance of tempest. The writer of Psalm 83 must have been familiar with this, as verse 15 shows: *"Thy tempest, Thy storm."* Fire, hail, snow, vapor, and stormy wind fulfilling His Word, is the language of Psalm 148:8.

How often the failure of an ostentatious military or naval scheme has been due to adverse weather. The storm that scattered the Armada, Russia's snows and Napoleon, the rain at Waterloo, are all instances of the hand of Providence in recent centuries. The present century, too, furnishes instance after instance of the intervention of the same hand. The snows of the winter of 1939-40 held up military movements and resulted in the preservation of human life in Finland and France. The unusual calm of the days of Dunkirk made possible the deliverance of many whose lives had appeared forfeit. This unusual calm contrasts with the sudden violent storms of September 1940, when the invasion of Britain was threatened. Sudden changes in weather conditions unaccountable to meteorology have occurred frequently, sometimes with serious, sometimes with merciful consequences.

(3) *Earthquakes:*

In the days of Moses an earthquake was a new thing, a singular means of showing divine displeasure in the engulfment of Korah, Dathan and Abiram (Num. 16:29-30). What was new then was repeated in the days of Uzziah (Zech. 14:5). But it has become more frequent as this age has drawn to its evening stages, the close of which will be marked by frequency and intensification of these shakings (Mt. 24:7; Rev. 11:13; Heb. 12:26).

(4) *Insect Pests:*

That which the palmerworm hath left hath the locust eaten, and that which the locust hath left hath the cankerworm eaten; and that which the cankerworm hath left hath the caterpillar eaten (Joel 1:4). (See also Deut. 28:38, 42; Amos 4:9; Ps. 78:45-46.)

The powerlessness of man against insect scourges has made nations both ancient and modern dread them. The nations of Canaan suffered in their bodies, and the Egyptians suffered in their crops. More than once Israel, too, found her fields stripped, and her oliveyards bare. Instances of modern pests and their ravages are too numerous to mention.

(5) *Wild Beasts:*

If I cause noisome beasts to pass through the land, and they spoil it, so that it be desolate, that no man may pass through because of the beasts (Ezek. 14:15).

The ravages of destructive beasts are better known in lands less developed and less populated than the countries of the West, but ancient and modern days provide many instances of this operation of Providence. The beasts that should be subject to man and over which man should rule, become rebellious and antagonistic to men who are not subject to God, and who show their rebellion and antagonism by their sin against Him.

The Lord Jesus was with the wild beasts during the temptation (Mk. 1:13) and rode an unbroken colt, but there was no insubjection or wildness with them then. The blessed One who was perfectly subject to the will of God enjoyed the dominion over the beasts, that belonged to man before the Fall. When fallen man rebels against God, he must not complain if God moves the beasts to rebel against him.

Balaam's ass provides a study in contrast with the Lord's ride into Jerusalem. Another marked instance is found, when, at Elisha's behest, the she bears from the wood tare the hostile city youths (not children), who, brought up in idolatry, railed on the faithful Elijah whom they and their parents had rejected. They spurned Elisha, the man of God, sent to be the *"salvation of Jehovah"* (the meaning of his name) to them and the nation.

(6) *Withholding Good Things:*

Your iniquities have turned away these things, and your sins have withholden good from you (Jer. 5:25).

When God created the earth, He selected Eden for man, spreading out its luxuriant garden, replete with everything to be desired. But man, having sinned, was driven out and denied the good things of Eden's blessings. In like manner, since the Fall, the good things of life are often withheld because of sin. The sunshine of blessing is taken out of life and replaced by the cloud of difficulty. The full provision that blesses honest labor gives place to meager return for the sweat of the brow.

The spirit of the first fourteen verses of Deuteronomy 28 might be contrasted with the spirit of the remaining portion of the chapter, in illustration of the fact that the good things given for obedience are withheld for disobedience, being replaced by a process of increasing sorrow.

As Solomon remarks, *"to the sinner God giveth travail"* (Eccl. 2:26). *"The way of transgressors is hard"* (Prov. 13:15).

(7) *Plague and Pestilence:*

The Lord shall make the pestilence cleave unto thee, until He have consumed thee from off the land, whither thou goest in to possess it. The Lord shall smite thee

117

with consumption, and with fever, and with inflamma-
tion, and with fiery heat, and the sword, and with blast-
ing, and with mildew; and they shall pursue thee until
thou perish...The Lord shall smite thee with the boil of
Egypt, and with the emerods, and with the scurvy, and
with the itch, whereof thou canst not be healed. The
Lord shall smite thee with madness, and blindness, and
astonishment of heart: and thou shalt grope at noon-
day, as the blind gropeth in darkness, and thou shalt
not prosper in thy ways: and thou shalt be only
oppressed and spoiled alway, and there shall be none
to save thee...If thou wilt not observe to do all the
words of this law that are written in this book, that
thou mayest fear this glorious and fearful name, THE
LORD THY GOD; then the Lord will make plagues
wonderful, and the plagues of thy seed, even great
plagues, and of long continuance, and sore sicknesses,
and of long continuance. He will bring upon thee again
all the diseases of Egypt, which thou wast afraid of;
and they shall cleave unto thee. Also every sickness,
and every plague, which is not written in the book of
this law, them will the Lord bring upon thee, until thou
be destroyed (Deut. 28:21-22, 27-29, 58-61).

Israel was threatened with being afflicted as other
nations had been by the dread maladies here mentioned.
It is awful to think that the world of germs, microbes and
bacilli may be used by God on rebel nations.

Historians of World War I do not hesitate to say that the
scourge of influenza played a major part in the fall of the

Kaiser's Germany, removing, as it eventually did, 12,000,000 souls from the earth in two years. It spread from Germany to lands afar, exceeding in its toll of mankind the 10,000,000 slain by the four-years' conflict.

The destruction of Sennacherib's host is an instance of the rapid destruction caused by a lightning plague, 185,000 men being removed in a night. What a defense the God of heaven was to Hezekiah, but what an enemy to the Assyrians who had magnified themselves against Him!

When the ark was among the Philistines, they were afflicted by tumors, until the cry of the city went up to heaven. Egypt's magicians and people of ancient days experienced the grievousness of this form of divine castigation, as will the ungodly of the last days, when the Apocalyptic vials are poured out (Rev. 16:2, 11).

The Spirit of God in the words of Zechariah 14:12 takes our thoughts to these last days, when some form of tuberculosis, working with almost lightning rapidity, will account for armies laying siege to Jerusalem.

The Lord Himself says that pestilences and plagues will be more frequent and severe in those days of multiplied iniquity, to which the human race draws near.

(8) *Unemployment Resulting from Godless Statesmanship; Divine Interference with Natural Supplies:*

Neither shall there be for Egypt any work, which head or tail, palm branch or rush, may do (Isa. 19:15).

A careful reading of Isaiah 19 will show that the politicians of Egypt who did not recognize God, formulated their economic policy, reckoning on the constant flow of the Nile. It is well known that Egypt depends little on the direct rainfall of heaven, but the Nile, bearing the waters from the great inland lakes and watersheds of Africa, looms large in the calculations of the Egyptian, being deified in the place of God. It is overlooked that the river, wherever it rises and however it is fed, depends, even if indirectly, on the mercy of God who gives the rain.

The chapter, speaking of those that fish in the Nile, those that sow in the meadows of the Nile, those that work in combed flax, and those that weave cotton, presents to us fisheries, agriculture, and manufacturing, all of which are confounded by the diminished flow of the great river. The finger of God controls the elements (Ps. 119:91), and, acting upon the main artery of their system, disappoints the schemes of the proud self-sufficient politicians of the land, making the princes of Zoan foolish and deceiving the princes of Noph.

The collapse of their schemes and the failure of their economic policy results in total unemployment, which affects the spirit and morale of the people, resulting in the fall of the state, and the subjugation of the nation to the foreign despot, described as a cruel lord.

All their consulting with wizards, seeking unto idols, charmers and those that have familiar spirits, avails nothing, and brings no relief in the day of their visitation.

The principles revealed in this passage should have a special voice to the nations today, because, whatever measure of fulfillment this chapter may have had in the past, it has never been completely fulfilled throughout, and therefore awaits its exhaustive fulfillment and consummation at the end of this age, when *"the transgressors have come to the full"* (Dan. 8:23; 11:42-43). A modern Egypt is its subject (see "Remnants" in the section on "The End of the Age"), the fall of which, under the oppression of the mighty Assyrian, will result in a remnant crying to God and being delivered at the coming of God's Christ and King, who shall reign to the glory of God and the blessing of the redeemed (lsa. 19:21).

(9) *Weak Morale—Indefiniteness and Fear:*

The fishers also shall lament, and all they that cast angle into the Nile shall mourn, and they that spread nets upon the waters shall languish. Moreover, they that work in combed flax, and they that weave white cloth, shall be ashamed...Neither shall there be for Egypt any work, which head or tail, palm branch or rush, may do (lsa. 19:8, 9, 15).

"The heart of Egypt shall melt" (v. 1), *"The spirit of Egypt shall be made void"* (v. 3), *"Egypt, like women...shall tremble and fear"* (v. 16), are terms that describe what would, in modern language, be called morale. This chapter provides incontestable evidence that morale is controlled by God; *"the God of the spirits of all flesh,"* who is as well able to affect the spirit of a nation as He is able to affect the bodies of its people. He can weaken the spirit of the proud, and righteously does so, when they vaunt their independence of Him and of the resource found in Him.

This weakened morale results in lack of cohesion in the state (v. 2), and the spirit of perverseness causes the leaders to err in their purposes.

(10) *Deprivation of Personal Freedom:*

For I will no more pity the inhabitants of the land, saith the Lord: but, lo, I will deliver the men every one into his neighbor's hand, and into the hand of his king: and they shall smite the land, and out of their hand I will not deliver them (Zech. 11:6).

The days of Joseph provide a clear instance of this, when, through famine, the state gained power over and possession of lands, crops, cattle, men and women, until all became the goods and chattels of the ruler. It appears that it was so directed of God, for it was He who gave the visions of the fat kine and lean kine, and of the good ears and thin ears, giving to Joseph, too, the ability to interpret and the wisdom to apply the revelation contained in the king's dream. Thus the people were delivered into the hand of the king and the state.

Surely if liberties and freedom are used in a sinful way it is righteous of God to restrain those liberties and curtail that freedom. The increasing power of the state is a mark of the end of the age, and an evidence of the approach of the day when Revelation 13:16 will be fulfilled internationally, and men will be unable to buy or sell without the badge of allegiance to the Empire and the evidence of homage to its Emperor.

What a responsibility the freedom of the Western

world puts upon both the Christian and the unbeliever! Will God continue to allow these privileges if they are continually abused?

(11) *Overthrow of a City, such as Sodom, Nineveh, Pompeii, and St. Pierre:*

The cities of the plain, where Lot vexed his righteous soul and made his testimony fruitless by compromise, were destroyed in spite of the intercessions of the friend of God. Thus began a long line of instances, which embraces the wicked Nineveh, Pompeii and St. Pierre down to the cities of our time, and which finds its climax in the mightiest catastrophe of all—when the new Babylon, the coming dream city of man on the banks of Euphrates, will be engulfed in a day, bearing its load of pleasure-drunk and sin-intoxicated men and women into eternity, after which its smoking chasm will remain throughout the thousand years of the reign of righteousness as a warning to the new generations born in that age.

(12) *War:*

Ho Assyrian, the rod of Mine anger, and the staff in their hand is Mine indignation! I will send him against a profane nation, and against the people of My wrath will I give him a charge to take the spoil, and to take the prey, and to tread them down like the mire of the streets. Howbeit he meaneth not so, neither doth his heart think so; but it is in his heart to destroy and cut off nations not a few. For he saith, Are not my princes all of them kings? Is not Calno as Carchemish? Is not

Hamath as Arpad? Is not Samaria as Damascus? As my hand hath found the kingdoms of the idols, and whose graven images did excel them of Jerusalem and of Samaria; shall I not, as I have done unto Samaria and her idols, so do to Jerusalem and her idols?

Wherefore it shall come to pass that when the Lord hath performed His whole work upon mount Zion and on Jerusalem, I will punish the fruit of the stout heart of the king of Assyria, and the glory of his high looks. For he hath said, By the strength of my hand I have done it, and by my wisdom; for I am prudent...Shall the axe boast against him that heweth therewith? Shall the saw magnify itself against him that shaketh it? As if a rod should shake them that lift it up, or as if a staff should lift up him that is not wood.

Therefore shall the Lord, the Lord of hosts, send among his (the Assyrians) fat ones leanness; and under his glory there shall be kindled a burning like the burning of fire (Isa. 10:5-16).

And the Lord raised up an adversary unto Solomon, Hadad the Edomite: he was of the king's seed in Edom...And God raised up another adversary unto him, Rezon the son of Eliada, which had fled from his lord, Hadadezer, king of Zobah (1 Ki. 11:14, 23).

And the Lord stirred up against Jehoram the spirit of the Philistines, and of the Arabians which are beside the Ethiopians (2 Chron. 21:16).

Or if I bring a sword upon that land, and say, Sword, go through the land; so that I cut off man and beast-from it (Ezek. 14:17).

These scriptures are but a fraction of the evidence found in the Word, showing that war is a divine visitation. The question is often asked, "Why does God allow this war?" It is not only true that God allows war, but these passages indicate that He directs war upon guilty nations.

Sometimes (as though God were unjust) the question is asked, "Why doesn't God stop the war?" Perhaps it is best answered by another question, "Why do not men stop their sins?" When Israel asked such questions as, *"Wherefore come these things upon me?"* (Jer. 13:22), God, who had anticipated the question, replies, *"Because of the multitude of thy sins," "Because thou hast forgotten Me."* When they ask, *"Wherefore hath the Lord done these things?"* they are told that it is because they have forsaken God.

Who will dare to say that the nations of Europe have been guiltless? Who will be so bold as to declare that Britain is innocent of moral, religious and political sin? When the so-called Christian ministry becomes traitor to the Bible that should be its guide, destroying it by hostile criticism, when in the land of Bibles children are reared in almost total ignorance of the Bible, when de-Christianized Europe embraces Buddhism, Islam and other oriental religions, and when Spiritism and Astrology are allowed to increase, and even true Christians avoid the pilgrim way, the question becomes

125

not "Why is there a war?" but "Why didn't it come before?" Not "Why are people killed?" but "Why so few comparatively?" When the sins of European nations are assessed and the consequences in the visitations of these sins counted, the mercy of God will become more conspicuous than the justice that brings upon men the sad happenings of these days.

In the historical books (Samuel, Kings and Chronicles), and in the Prophets, instances abound of war coming as the result of moral decline. The most striking is found in the experience of Solomon, Israel's most peaceable and richest monarch. When Solomon built up his long succession of sins to a height that demanded divine action, we read, *"The Lord stirred up an adversary unto Solomon"* (1 Ki. 11:14). The man of peace, after a reign of peace, had war brought upon himself. The twenty-third verse of the same chapter and 1 Chronicles 5:26 concur to emphasize that war is a divine visitation.

The expressions occurring in Isaiah 10 about the Assyrian aggressor are plain and unequivocal. He is called, *"the Rod of Mine anger."* Again God says that *"the staff in their hand is Mine indignation,"* and *"I will send him against an hypocritical nation."*

This is more than war "allowed," it is war directed providentially as the expression of the wrath of God against the nation of Israel for their hypocrisy. So much profession, which condemned their practices, demanded that they should be spoiled and become a prey, and required, too, that they should be trodden down by the Assyrian victor.

Though this monarch was providentially raised up of God and moved against Israel, it is evident by the words, *"he meaneth not so, neither doth his heart think so,"* that he did not do the will of God intelligently, nor did he intend to do God's will. His ambition was only to destroy and cut off nations, thus gaining power and position in the earth. The arrogant ambition of this purpose and the pride of his heart God eventually punished. So, while the mills of God ground Israel, they also ground Israel's enemy in God's own time.

For the time the Assyrian was part of the powers that were ordained of God, in turn being deposed as God delegated authority in the earth and power over the nations to others. In ancient days, God used the Assyrian as His rod upon a number of nations and, having completed His work, He broke His rod. May not God form other rods of power-hungry men to chastise in like manner the guilty people of Europe and America? Furthermore, may He not break His rod when He has finished His work?

The Scriptures teach that God puts the sword of justice into the hand of the magistrate, who is called a sacred minister of God for the purpose of putting down crime in his own realm (Rom. 13:1-7). In like manner it seems that God puts the sword into the hand of one monarch to chastise another and raises one nation to power to accomplish His visitation upon the sinning nation it subjugates.[1]

(13) *Despotism Allowed:*

And the Egyptians will give over into the hand of a

127

cruel lord; and a fierce king shall rule over them, saith the Lord, the Lord of hosts (Isa. 19:4).

The only way to deal with Egypt was to put them under the dominance of the Assyrians, and to shut them up to his power, so that, all help of man being cut off, they should cry to God, whom previously they had ignored, so that they should be delivered by His mercy.

A people's affliction, even though that affliction be a visitation, is a ground of appeal to the Lord, whose ways embrace lovingkindness as well as judgment.

This was true of Israel in Egypt. Who knows how much its principle may be operative at present in the affairs of the nations of Europe? Their sins came up and cried for visitation. Visitation has come, over-taking nation after nation, bringing death and destruction, pain and misery, removing liberties, resulting in oppression, denying the necessities of life, and causing disease. The cycle moves slowly, the cry of affliction rises. Not that the cry of sin has ceased, but, as the cry of the afflicted increases in volume and there is some repentance, He who delights in mercy will hear and spare. May the afflicted, in repentance, cry sincerely to Him, and may the godly, as they pray, remember that they have a ground of appeal on behalf of all men (1 Tim. 2:1) not only for their salvation, but also for their circumstances.

(14) *Loss of National Position; Dispersal among other Nations:*

And Moab shall be destroyed from being a people,

because he hath magnified himself against the Lord (Jer. 48:42).

My God will cast them away, because they did not hearken unto him: and they shall be wanderers among the nations (Hosea 9:17).

These quotations are so clear in themselves as not to require remark: Israel is the notable example. Many other nations that held power in ancient days have passed from the horizon of affairs, though some of them will reappear in power at the end of this age.

Loss of political status, limitation of national power, even loss of national position, come as the consequences of political sin. Affliction of people, deprivation of the good things of life, infliction of evil things, follow religious and moral misbehavior.

It is often said that the God of the Old Testament is quite different in character from the God of the New Testament. We have seen, however, that as to His governmental ways and providential dealings He is the same. The view that God is all love—a tolerant, indulgent, accommodating Being—is a mistaken one, having no resemblance to the God of the Bible. Embraced today in the character of God are all those features, completely unchanged through time. But God is a moral Being, holy and righteous, who governs according to abiding principles. He hates sin and punishes the wicked.

Yet we shall find that "behind a frowning providence He hides a smiling face," for all the while His moral government operates with a view to the accomplishment of purposes of redemption.

If this chapter were our last, there might be a danger of such a partial view of God as the people of Melita had when they spoke of God only as Vengeance. So we proceed to our next chapter and consider the principles of the ways of God, observing not only the dark cloud but the bow of mercy and its variegated beauties. Though He takes vengeance, He is no more only vengeance than He is only compassion. His perfect character is a harmonious blend and an exact balance of every feature. This was perfectly expressed in the Lord Jesus, who is God manifested in flesh. He was marked by firmness without hardness, gentleness without softness, love without sentiment, precision without mechanicalness, consideration without compromise, sympathy without indulgence, promptness without haste, burning zeal without ruthlessness, hatred of sin without hatred of the sinner, rebuke without vindictiveness, and a thousand more virtues without any of their corresponding vices. All such virtues are the glory of the unchangeable God seen in the face of Jesus Christ.

ENDNOTE:

1 There is a difference to be observed between Gentile monarchs being moved providentially to castigate others and those occasions where Jewish leaders such as Moses, Joshua, Gideon, David and others, were directly commanded by God to execute judgment intelligently.

CHAPTER TEN

The Principles of Divine Visitation

The Sweet Singer of Israel, reviewing the works of God, says, *"He made known His ways unto Moses, His acts unto the children of Israel"* (Ps. 103:7). We have been considering some of the acts of God in the preceding chapter, the isolated actions and outward evidences of Him. Here we think about His ways in the affairs of nations. His acts merely recount what God is doing; His ways unfold why such events occur.

With those who see only His acts, it has become common, almost popular, to question God and find fault with His dealings with men. Some dare to go as far as the Israelites did in the days of Ezekiel and say, *"The way of the Lord is not equal"* (Ezek. 18:29). But the Israelites' ideas of Him were perverted by the unequal character of their own ways. So, beholding His doings with astigmatic vision, they read their own evil into what they saw of God. Mistaking longsuffering for tolerance, warnings for threatenings, forgiveness for indulgence, judgment for antagonism, they arrived at a mistaken idea of God. Their God was a god of their imagination, a being altogether different from what God really is. They missed the fact that, without tolerating sin, He, in longsuffering forbears the sinner. In the meantime, He warns so that the sinner may repent, and is ready to forgive when that repentance is real. If that longsuffering, warning, waiting, forgiveness, goes unheeded, He must execute the sentence that might righteously have been inflicted at the first.

They blamed Him for being (in their view) an ogre, instead of praising Him for being beneficent and all-wise, as He really is. May He in some measure do for us as He did for Moses, make known to us His ways, granting us right thoughts of Himself from His Word. Our responsibility is to give Him our undivided attention and to be ready to adjust our thoughts to the facts of revelation.

As we proceed, we shall find more than a dozen easily discerned principles governing the acts of God with mankind.

(1) *The Necessity of Visitation:*

The visitations of God are necessary to the existence and experience of the human race. Earth's cries for the hand of God are many. A few of these cries will come before us here, to demonstrate this principle. *"The voice of thy brother's blood crieth unto ME."* This was a cry to God for justice against Cain. The cry of Sodom coming up before God was the cry of sin. The voice of the affliction of Israel enslaved in Egypt became loud in the ears of God, who is moved by the groans of the oppressed. In

New Testament days, James tells of unpaid wages crying to God to the accompaniment of the voice of the deprived laborers (Jas. 5:4).

It was necessary to the instruction of the succeeding generations for God to intervene by branding Cain, who thus bore witness to God's displeasure and became a warning against the sin of murder. Accompanying the branding and banishment of the unrepentant Cain was the giving of Seth as a comfort for the bereaved parents.

An awful exposure of Sodom results from the glimpse we get of its moral character when the angels sent in mercy would have been made the victims of unmentionable sin. Who will dare to suppose that it is good for the human race that such sinners should remain to pollute the moral atmosphere of man? It is necessary that they should be exterminated as the Canaanites were in after years. The cry of Sodom's sin must be answered for man's sake by the removal of the inhabitants of the plain.

The God of perfect courtesy and decorum chose Moses, brought up as a prince at the Egyptian court, refined by the years of patience *"perfect work"* in the obscure depths of the desert, and sent him with a reasonable request to Pharaoh, desiring no more than a few days' holiday (Ex. 5:1) for the enslaved people. When it is remembered that Joseph was the salvation of the land, the preserver of the very state that Pharaoh afterwards ruled, the grace of God to Pharaoh is magnified as God acts for the unrighteously oppressed people.

But when such a simple request is refused, such courtesy churlishly turned aside, it is necessary that Pharaoh be taught that oppression can be no longer tolerated. The groaning must cease. If Pharaoh will be so foolish as to obstruct the wheels of God's providence for Israel, He must not blame God because he is crushed by them as they roll onward in the path of justice. But though he is crushed, the very publicity of it (for the news spread far, see Josh. 2:10) becomes a warning to other nations. Rahab is saved as a result (Josh. 2:8-21), and who can tell how many will be in heaven as a result of the preaching of the story of the Passover? As well, redeemed Israel became a moral salt among the nations by what they learned of God through His operations toward them.

Had not God swept away all humanity at the Flood, sparing the only family pure in its generation, the whole race would have lost its human character, becoming corrupted into something other than man. Had not God utterly destroyed the wicked inhabitants of Canaan by the sword of Joshua and Israel, they would soon have sunken to the level of beasts. For while it cannot be true that the beast evolves into the human, the human can sink to be indistinguishable from the beast, even becoming guilty of sins that beasts would not practice.

Just as salt is needed to arrest corruption, so divine visitation is essential, acting as a righteous check on sin, in mercy delivering the oppressed, and ensuring the continuance of orderly conditions of human life. These visitations operate as God reveals Himself in the course of human history. He thus brings into view His purposes of redemption and a new creation, until at last we come to a *"new heaven and a new earth,"* in which there will be neither sin nor groan, neither tears nor death, and the universe will thrill with the praise of God and the Lamb.

> *"The new creation's stainless joy*
> *Gleams through the present gloom;*
> *That world of bliss without alloy,*
> *The saints' eternal home."*

(2) *Investigation:*

"The Lord came down to see" (Gen. 11:5). *"The cry of Sodom and Gomorrah is great...I will go down now and see"* (Gen. 18:20-21). Such passages furnish evidence that God Himself carefully investigates the character, circumstances, and degree of sin before visitation comes.

The words *"I will not revoke its sentence"* (Amos 1:3, 6, 9, 11, 13; 2:1, 4, 6, DARBY) indicate a court where evidence has been heard, decision arrived at, and sentence passed. In the Scriptures court scenes in heaven are suggested from which, after careful investigation, apportioning the guilt, and weighing the circumstances with all attendant causes and features, the visitation proceeds.

Daniel's fourth chapter tells of watchers, heaven's watchers of earth's behavior, who meet in heaven's court, where God sits greatly to be feared in the secret council of the Holy Ones (Ps. 89:7, NEWBERRY marg. and DARBY). All those that are about Him have Him in reverence as He from the Throne, founded on justice and judgment, sends forth lovingkindness and truth before His face, ruling the raging of the sea and directing heaven and earth (see Ps. 89:5-14).

135

The court scenes of Daniel 7 and Revelation 4 and 5 are well known to the Bible lover. They depict future scenes of investigation of earth's guilt on the one hand and Christ's worth on the other, and result in the destruction of earth's powers and in the sovereignty of the Lamb in the world where He was crucified. Reference to the following passages will provide further confirmation of this principle: *"The Judge of all the earth"* (Gen. 18:25), *"The Lord the Judge"* (Jud. 11:27), *"I am He which searcheth the reins* (from *renes*, the kidneys, organs of purification and so treated as the seat of motives, *ed.*) *and hearts"* (Rev. 2:23).

(3) *Recompense:*

...for the Lord God of recompenses, He shall surely requite (Jer. 51:56)

There is a sense in which men by their actions ask for, in fact, demand the recompense of Heaven.

The word recompense is frequent in Ezekiel. It occurs no less than nine times. Joel 3:7 says, *"I...will return your recompense upon your own head."* Isaiah 59:18 states, *"According to their deeds accordingly He will repay,"* and Obadiah 15 promises, *"thy reward in the shall return upon thine own head"* (DARBY). Thus the prophets unite to use language which substantiates the statement of the New Testament: *"receiving in themselves that recompense of their error which was meet"* (Rom. 1:27).

We are warned not to allow ourselves to be deceived,

for God is not mocked, *"Whatsoever a man soweth that shall he also reap"* (Gal. 6:7). The labor of sowing and the value of the seed is paid for in the harvest. If men labor to sow sin, they will reap its wages. *"According to their deeds accordingly He will repay."* The character of their behavior will be paid in the coin of Heaven; here and now in circumstances upon earth the ways of men will be recompensed upon their own heads (see Jer. 4:18).

(4) *Poetic Justice:*

Much akin to our previous section comes this one, showing that there is a balance between the character of the sin and the character of the visitation. The Philistines spared no remnant of their enemies, in return for which no remnant of them was spared (Am. 1:6-8). Israel's temple had been desolate of real worship to God; it was therefore made desolate in visitation (Mic. 6:13; 7:13). Famine, which allows so little to man, is often the result of man having given so little to God.

"As thou hast done, it shall be done to thee," says Obadiah 15. They had no pity for God's sanctuary, so God in turn withdraws His pity from them. Because they refuse to hear Him speaking through His prophets He refuses to hear them when they pray (Mic. 3:4; Jer. 11:11, 14). They rage against Him, only to find His rage against them (Isa. 37:28-29; Hos. 7:16). It is truly said of God, *"with the froward Thou wilt show Thyself froward"* (Ps. 18:25-27). The following passages support this principle: Ps. 62:12; Jer. 17:10; 2 Chron. 6:23; Ez. 11:21; 16:43; 23:49; 24:14; Obad. vv. 14-15; ls. 1:15.

(5) *Process or Cycle:*

As there is time of harvest after sowing, so there is time of visitation after sinning. The familiar cycle of the seasons illustrates the cycle of Providence. The result of sin is not seen immediately, but its actions are like seed sown, which appears to lie dormant awhile, yet grows relentlessly to its own kind of harvest at its own time. Actions and ways are like a boomerang coming back to us in circumstances of like character.

"Thy doom is come unto thee" (Ezek. 7:7), *"Thy doom is gone forth"* (Ezek. 7:10), are the words of Ezekiel to Israel. As he speaks he uses a significant expression (found only here in the Bible) which means the cycle or the turn, or, as Fuerst has put it, "the revolution of fortune, giving the idea of reciprocal motion, the going out of actions, the return of circumstances."

Many say that the sorrow that follows sin is simply the result of natural processes, but the questions come: Who designed the processes? Who made them natural? Who has sustained their working during these six thousand years of human history? That they are the revolution of a cycle, the working of a process, is true, but that God designed the cycle and operates the revolution of fortune governing the processes that He designed is also true, and converging under His hand they produce a time of visitation.

It would seem that in the coming age, when the personal rule of Christ on earth will be known, the cycle of operation will be accelerated. The sins of those born in that age will then be visited immediately by death, and deficiency in worship by immediate famine (see Zech. 14:17-19).

(6) *Partial Punishment:*

It has been proven that God does punish sin here and now in life and circumstances. But that punishment of sin is by no means the complete payment of it. It is as true that God never fully punishes as it is true that He does punish (Ps. 103:9). Isaiah explains the reason for this when God says that *"the spirit should fail before me, and the souls which I have made"* (Isa. 57:16). If God were to rise up and meet every human sin and every iniquity of man with its full punishment, soon mankind would cease to exist on the earth. None would be exempt; all merit punishment, for none are without failure and sin. Men would be worn away by the recurring pressure for each repeated sin. The existence of men and the ordered life of earth is therefore a monument to the mercy of God, who, though He visits sin, does not yet fully punish it.

(7) *Discrimination:*

The visitations of God operate neither blindly nor brutally. The wheels of His providential government are *"full of eyes"* (Ezek. 1:18). Discrimination and discernment mark all His ways. He can plague Egypt with darkness and at the same time give Israel light in their dwellings. He can rock the prison and reduce the jailer to terror, while Paul and Silas, singing praises to God, find that the earthquake breaks their stocks without harming them.

139

The fires of heaven consume the cities of the plain, but not until Lot is removed to a place of safety. Belshazzar is slain on a fateful night, but the godly Daniel is not only preserved, but given a place in the new regime. Nebuchadnezzar sins as a king and suffers as a king, but his state, statesmen, and peoples seem to be unaffected. The government of Darius, which made laws against the godly, are cast into the very den of lions that they intended for Daniel, while Darius, Daniel, the state and people, innocent of these sins, escape. When a state sins as a state it appears that God deals with it in that capacity; and when the people sin as a people, they themselves reap the consequences in their personal circumstances. Guilty cities seem to be dealt with as cities, being visited as cities and sometimes being completely overthrown.

From Genesis to Revelation, Scripture abounds in evidence of the discriminating character of the doings of God. When the apocalyptic judgments are in the earth and the trumpets sound, the third part of the earth will be peculiarly affected, the more severe judgments being concentrated on the more guilty part, while the less guilty two-thirds will sustain lighter chastisement.

But someone will say, and rightly too, that this discrimination does not secure immunity for the godly, for they are affected by the visitations of God, suffering it would seem almost needlessly. Job, Daniel, Ezekiel and the Thessalonians are some examples. Here we need discrimination and discernment.

Daniel suffered in the visitation that fell on his guilty people, exiled from his land, deprived of the worship of

Jehovah's temple, robbed of the privilege of marriage and family life, removed to the strange, ungodly court. In like manner, Ezekiel lost much in the same series of visitations. The second Epistle of Paul to the Thessalonians found them suffering tribulation because of the righteous judgment of God on the people of the area where they lived. Job, too, was stripped of all by the very means that God uses to punish the ungodly. His friends were convinced that he was a hypocrite exposed and suffering for his previous secret sins. But there is a difference which emphasizes the discriminating character of God's ways.

When He allows the godly to suffer, it is not for the same reason nor with the same object as when He visits the ungodly. Job's friends, though evidently well instructed in the ways of God's government with the world, were ignorant of the fact that God causes the godly to suffer for the development of virtue rather than the punishment of evil. Already living on so high a plane of righteousness as to be a testimony in heaven, Job was lifted to a higher plane of experience as he submitted to the hand of God. His friends insisted, in spite of everything, that the righteous man merited the punishment of God because of his sins. But when the cycle was complete, the friends were directed to seek Job's intercession on their behalf.

He who had sustained in patience so much trial, proved the blessing of the Lord in the end, and became a benediction to those very friends who had so mistaken him.

Though Daniel had lost much, he gained more, being immeasurably enriched in spiritual power and in the revelation of the mind of God and His purposes. Thus he

stands out as one of the greatest and most effective intercessors of all time. His writings are the key to all prophecy; his prayers affect nations past and future; his godliness is a pattern, whether as the obscure exile or as the
counselor of Nebuchadnezzar's court, whether unrecog-
nized by Belshazzar or called to interpret the writing, or
among the new order of the Persian power. He stands out
as the man of character and accomplishment, one of the
nobles of God's kingdom who will *"stand in thy lot at the
end of the days."* All these spiritual abilities and moral
qualities were developed by his experiences during the
visitation on his nation and will be rewarded by a special
place in the kingdom of Christ, not to speak of the material things that accompanied his high station in the three
successive courts.

When circumstances of trial came upon the surrounding people as a *"token of the righteous judgment of God"*
(2 Thess. 1:5), the Thessalonian believers in their midst
suffered too. Their tribulation was added to by the attitude of the world, who, under the visitation, vented their
rancor in persecuting the Christians. Nevertheless the
deep and costly experience enriched the people of God
and served to fit them for the glory to which they were
destined.

If God, as He visits nations today, has allowed the
Christian reader to suffer, be assured that the compensa-
tions will outweigh the losses that might be his.
Whenever His people pass through the fires they may
learn the communion of the Son of God who will walk
with them, and they find that the flames consume only

THE PRINCIPLES OF DIVINE VISITATION

the things that hitherto bound them. (See *Appendix* on "The Suffering of Believers.)

(8) *Revelational:*

In an earlier section we observed the "poetic justice" of the consequences that human sin brings upon itself, and from this we learn something further. The congruity between the visitation and the sin that occasions it brings out into the light the evil that is hidden in the soul. The fruit shows the character of the root, the harvest the nature of the seed. James says that sin, *"when it is finished, bringeth forth death."* Sin is the seed of death and the process of sin is the process of death.

God made Israel's temple desolate, so revealing and making public what Israel had become—a ruin, desolate of spiritual value to God. The barrenness and waste of famine exposes the condition of man as barren and waste before God because of the sins that deserve the famine. The antagonism of war shows the antagonism of the heart of man toward God. The visitations of God are a mirror of the souls of men and circumstances of national experience a portrait of the people as viewed from heaven.

(9) *Waiting:*

How often does the Scripture emphasize that God is slow to anger! Because of His great longsuffering, He resorts to visitation only when there is no other remedy. This is shown in the case of Sodom, Jerusalem, Nineveh, Babylon, and many other cities.

The phrase of Amos 1 and 2 already referred to indicates this. The language is not, *"I will punish,"* but *"I will not turn away the sentence."* Even after investigation resulting in righteous sentence, God waits before the execution of that sentence. He is not in a hurry to punish the sinner. Indeed, the only time there is suggestion of haste with God is in the picture of the father who runs to the repentant son to cover him with the kisses of forgiveness. Space for repentance is always allowed by the longsuffering One who is *"slow to anger"* but *"ready to pardon."*

(10) **Warning:**

"The Lord God will do nothing, (until) *He revealeth His secret unto His servants the prophets"* (Amos 3:7). How full of warning was the ministry of the prophets in their day! God, who waits before the execution of His sentence, even goes the length of warning, that those deserving wrath may be the objects of mercy.

Warning was a distinct feature of the preaching of the Lord Jesus. He warned of the wrath of God in human circumstances on earth (Lk. 13:3, 5) as clearly as He warned of the wrath of God *"where their worm dieth not and the fire is not quenched"* (Mk. 9:48).

All the messengers of the gospel used warning with their message (Acts 17:31). God's visitations never take advantage of men; judgments come unheralded only after warnings have been unheeded.

It is true that some of the plagues of Egypt fell without warning. The third one of each of the three sets of three was unheralded because the warnings accompanying the previous ones were unheeded.

(11) *Repentance:*

The generosity and grace of God's character is seen in the fact that when men repent of their sins, He repents of the chastisement due to them and about to fall.

This is so plainly said in Jeremiah 18:7-11, that there is hardly need to turn elsewhere. The words are:

At what instant I shall speak concerning a nation, and concerning a kingdom, to pluck up and to break down and to destroy it; if that nation, concerning which I have spoken, turn from their evil, I will repent of the evil that I thought to do unto them. And at what instant I shall speak concerning a nation and concerning a kingdom, to build and to plant it; if it do evil in My sight, that it obey not My voice, then I will repent of the good, wherewith I said I would benefit them. Now, therefore, go to, speak to the men of Judah, and to the inhabitants of Jerusalem, saying, Thus saith the Lord; Behold, I frame evil against you, and devise a device against you: return ye now every one from his evil way, and amend your ways and your doings.

We are familiar with the operation of the first part of this regarding the city of Nineveh, the destruction of which was averted by the repentance of its people. The principle working in the inverse order operated regarding Israel, who because of sin forfeited purposed blessing so many times (see Isa. 30:15, 18). The passage is not limited to Israel or to any other nation; it applies to all. Its principle operates in two directions. Turning from evil will avert national disaster, but turning to evil will equally result in a change of the purpose of good. He who withholds purposed evil when the people repent, turning from sin, will withhold purposed good if the people turn to evil, rejecting His word.

This principle emphasizes national responsibility, embracing the whole constitution, statesmen and legislators, the rank and file. The passing of laws to permit sins in war time will result in greater difficulties. The call to repentance and prayer will be followed by alleviation of distress. Yet if, upon some alleviation and respite, there is ingratitude, forgetfulness and turning to further sin, we may expect the process of alleviation to cease and further troubles to befall the nation.

(12) *Mercy:*

The well-known words of classic English express a great principle:

> *The quality of mercy is not strained,*
> *It droppeth as the gentle rain from heaven*
> *Upon the place beneath: it is twice blessed,*
> *It blesseth him that gives, and him that takes:*
> *'Tis mightiest in the mightiest; it becomes*
> *The throned monarch better than his crown;*
> *His scepter shows the force of temporal power,*
> *The attribute to awe and majesty,*
> *Wherein doth sit the dread and fear of kings,*
> *But mercy is above this sceptered sway,*
> *It is enthroned in the hearts of kings,*
> *It is an attribute to God Himself.*

(Wm. Shakespeare, *Merchant of Venice,* 4:1)

Mercy is exalted above the force of temporal power, the awe and majesty of kings. This mighty quality, filling the Bible as it does, is prominent in all the movings of Providence. God rarely acts without mercy. A whole Psalm (136) is dedicated to show how it is interwoven with the acts of God. Provision of food (v. 25), deliverance from enemies (v. 24), even the removal of Pharaoh (v. 15), Sihon (v. 19), and Og (v. 20) and the creation of heaven and earth are connected with the outflow of His abiding mercy.

James, conveying in a sentence the superiority of mercy, says, *"mercy glorieth against judgment"* (Jas. 2:13), showing that it operates on a higher plane than judgment. The judgment of God operates on the plane of justice, but God delights to be generous, acting on the higher plane of mercy and lovingkindness. How much better that Nineveh be spared than judged! How much better that those 120,000 children were spared! The judgment of God overthrowing the wicked city would have been just; but how magnificent the preservation of the city upon their repentance!

The prophet's strong legalism prevented his rising to the heights of the magnificence of mercy, and caused him to be disappointed when Nineveh was not overthrown. Misguided, he reproached God for His highest quality when he said,

I knew that Thou art a gracious God, and full of compassion, slow to anger, and plenteous in mercy, and repentest Thee of the evil (Jon. 4:2).

147

But David's delighting heart sang, as thrilled in spirit he beheld the ways of God:

The Lord is gracious and full of compassion, slow to anger, and of great mercy. The Lord is good to all: and His tender mercies are over all His works (Ps. 145:8-9).

Even in the just visitation of the awful World Wars, when men on battlefield and on the sea, women and children in their homes, have been overtaken by violent death, the mercy of God is to be seen. Careful investigation will show it to be much more prominent than a passing glance might suggest. The miraculous preservation of life in the United Kingdom during World War II numbered more than the deaths. In fact the number of those killed by bombing was comparatively small in regard to the thousands of tons of explosives used. It has been said that there were as few deaths as only one to every twelve tons of bombs dropped. Surely we should have expected more. Is not this the mercy of God? If it is not the mercy of God, it is incumbent on the objector to give a better reason for the small proportion.

It would require a large library to set forth the many instances of divine mercy in one day of these hostilities, let alone during the course of the years. Why nine months of war without bombing? Why five days of calm at Dunkirk? Why was the only pier not destroyed though aimed at thousands of times? A school playground full of children was sprayed with machine-gun bullets, but not a child was hurt. A landmine exploded in a barrack full of marines, and not a man was hurt. Scores of such things could be quoted from the writer's experience, to say nothing of the much wider experience of some. For none of these miracles can one find a satisfactory reason except in the exercise of that superb quality, the **mercy** of God.

(13) *Progress of Intensity:*

In the courts of justice it is usual for a first offender to receive lenient treatment. Upon persistence in the particular breach of law he is more firmly dealt with; still further lawlessness is usually followed by the full extent of justice. This process can be seen at work in the ways of God with nations.

Two classic passages may be called to bear their witness that God increases the severity of chastisement when there is persistence in sin. The passages are Leviticus 26:14 to the end and Amos 4:6-13. The first sets forth what God said He would do to Israel if they refused to repent at His milder methods. The second, which we consider here, shows God reviewing a course of visitation which has grown in intensity because it has failed to produce repentance. In the end He warns them to prepare for severest judgment.

First of all plentiful provision of food is reduced to lack of bread. *"Yet have ye not returned unto Me, saith the Lord"* (Amos 4:6). Then the rain is withheld and water becomes scarce. *"Yet have ye not returned unto Me, saith the Lord"* (v. 8). The crops are smitten, gardens, vineyards, oliveyards are affected. *"Yet have ye not returned unto Me, saith the Lord"* (v. 9). Eventually pestilences come, followed by the sword, filling the land with the slain. But still the word is, *"Yet have ye not returned unto Me, saith the Lord"* (v. 10).

Finally, in the overthrow of their cities God miraculously saves some as firebrands plucked from the burning, but all with the same result. The lament is repeated for the fifth time. *"Yet have ye not returned unto Me, saith the Lord."* Now they are warned to meet God—to receive still severer judgment. So it always follows: if the lighter strokes are unheeded, heavier will fall.

The advice God gives is surely fitting in any day. *"Seek not Bethel, nor Gilgal, nor Beersheba, but seek ye ME."* Seek not places, however historically religious, but seek the living Person, the Creator of all things, who can make life dawn out of the darkness of death and who strengthens the spoiled against the strong. *"Seek good,"* is His advice, *"that ye may live in His world"* (Amos 5:4-14).

Israel and Judah passed through increasing degrees of visitation for their hardness of heart (2 Ki. 17:1-24; 2 Chron. 36:14-21). Many other nations, too, are spoken of who come under this process because of lack of the wisdom that results in repentance, humility, and confession.

It hardly needs to be pointed out that such increasing suffering of nations is needless if men will repent. God has no pleasure therein. The other principles discussed prove that His delight is in mercy and forgiveness (Ps. 130:4).

(14) ***Hire:***

Son of man, Nebuchadnezzar, King of Babylon, caused his army to serve a great service against Tyre: every head was made bald, and every shoulder was peeled: yet had he no wages, nor his army, from Tyre, for his service that he had served against it: therefore thus saith the Lord God: Behold, I will give the land of Egypt unto Nebuchadnezzar king of Babylon; and he shall carry off her multitude, and take her spoil, and take her prey; and it shall be the wages for his army. I have given him the land of Egypt as his recompence for which he served, because they wrought for Me, saith the Lord God" (Ezek. 29:18-20).

It has been shown in a previous chapter that God providentially moves one monarch against another, executing His censure and carrying out His purpose. Nebuchadnezzar was used to chastise a number of nations in his day. Conspicuous among them was Tyre, the proud city of craftsmanship and merchandise. Long had the pride of Tyre called for humbling. Its kings had changed since the reign of Hiram who was a lover of David (1 Ki. 5:1) and its people were different from what they were when they produced Hiram, the artisan (1 Ki. 7:13-14), who labored in the work of the temple in Solomon's day. Their cultivation of human genius, resulting in superior craftsmanship and commercial success, had made them think that their position among the nations was secure. Safe in their city which they believed impregnable, and forgetting God, their thoughts of themselves had become so exaggerated that their pride amounted to deification of the Tyrians.

It was a real service to man and to God to humble the

proud and complacent inhabitants of Tyre. God does not hesitate to say this, going even further and paying Nebuchadnezzar hire for doing so.

Just about the time of the fall of Tyre, after its long and costly siege, Egypt merited chastisement for its behavior. So Egypt, with its riches, was handed over to Nebuchadnezzar as his wages and the wages of his army for the signal service of humbling Tyre; the latter had yielded no spoil because of its complete destruction.

God is no man's debtor. If monarchs, even unconsciously, carry out the governmental purposes of God they will be paid for their service, as also in due course they will be paid for their sins.

The "Rod of Europe" seems to have been paid in spoil for his service upon not a few guilty nations. But as surely as this is true will he in due course be paid for his sins.

(15) *Balance of Account:*

The more we read the Scriptures and consider the ways of God with nations, the clearer does it become that the rise and fall of kingdoms is governed by moral and spiritual principles.

The political conduct of the state, the religious and moral behavior of a people, and the condition of the godly in their midst, are the things that really decide the fortunes of the state and the fate of its people.

If we could fully assess, as God does with perfect knowledge, the moral condition and behavior of nations we might be able to estimate the issues of conflict. But though we cannot do this there may be pointers, indications of how things will go in times of stress. A state which has multiplied political sin may be expected to suffer more than its opponent state, which, though not innocent, may be less guilty in this respect. A state that has been guilty of constitutional action against Christian truths will surely be dealt with more severely than another state that has not been thus guilty. A state that has passionately hated the Jews, unscrupulously and violently persecuting them, will surely stand in a different position from a state that has been a refuge for the persecuted and a harbor for the stranger.

The government that tears up treaty after treaty, riding roughshod over the obstacle of fidelity, will stand lower in moral account than one which honors its covenants.

When the leaders of a state constitutionally recognize God as the God of the governmental realm, and other leaders of other states as publicly deny Him, it may prove suggestive of the fortunes of these states.

If spiritual and moral matters weigh so much, surely the greatest benediction the believer can convey to the nation among which he lives, is his spiritual and moral influence. This influence is always strongest when he is farthest in heart from the world and its fever, and when he is nearest the Lord in the path of genuine Christian obedience.

APPENDIX: *The Suffering of Believers*

In regard to the mystery of the sufferings of believers much help is to be derived from Peter, both from his mistaken idea of suffering in his early days, and from the later words of a ripened experience. In the early stages of his spiritual life, suffering was an enigma to him; he was appalled at the idea of his beloved Master becoming subject to it, and in his natural zeal attempted to dissuade Him from the very *"hour"* for which He had come into the world. This drew forth the sharp rebuke which exposed the origin of the words so expressive of human sentiment (Mk. 8:31-38).

But it is a very different Peter who years afterwards wrote the Epistles, for in the first of them the Lord is presented as an example of suffering, in the path of which the believer is to follow His steps (1 Pet. 2:21-24).

It is to be expected that Peter will instruct his readers further in this great issue concerning which he has gained a radically different outlook. Nor does he disappoint this expectation, for he deals widely on the subject of suffering, outlining the spheres in which it may be encountered, suggesting various forms of it, and explaining the results it secures in those that are subjected to it.

He shows that the believer may suffer in the world at the hand of an employer, the state or the unconverted of the world. The overbearing master may unjustly cause grief to the believer, who is encouraged to bear it patiently (1 Pet. 2:18-21). The believer's right living may even be the cause of the worldling's hatred (1 Pet. 2:11-12), and result in vilification.

The murderer, thief, evil-doer and meddler obviously suffer at the hand of the magistrate for their evil behavior (Rom. 13:4). But not infrequently, suffering has been imposed by the *"powers that be"* on the people of God for their distinctively Christian behavior.

It may also be inferred that in the home a saved partner may suffer because of an unconverted one or because of an inconsiderate converted partner (1 Pet. 3:1-7).

The Church, too, may become a sphere of suffering because of unwilling, mercenary, or overbearing shepherds, who may cause great anxiety to younger believers, in fact to all the flock (see 1 Pet. 5:1-9).

Not only does Peter take for granted that suffering will occur in these circles, but he explains something of the various causes of suffering. He declares that the converted reap what they sow (1 Pet. 3:10-12). Having been called to *"inherit a blessing,"* believers may, as the result of evil, find the face of the Lord against them, and thus reap disciplinary suffering. The Corinthians are an example of this (1 Cor. 11:30).

But even so, there is no encouragement to interpret a brother's misfortune as discipline, for equally unmistakably it is declared that suffering can arise from totally different causes.

It is evident that righteousness and well-doing in a maladjusted world may bring about suffering for the believers as it did for their Lord, of whom it was declared by heaven, earth, and hell that He was without fault (1 Pet. 3:13-17).

Purely Christian behavior, such as the love of enemies and the doing of good to those that hate (so impossible to the unconverted), has often been mistaken for weakness, and sometimes for worse—for treachery. Instances abound in the long centuries of the Church's history, when states have demanded that Christians should do that which the principles of their high-calling prohibit. Having chosen to *"obey God rather than men,"* they have suffered inconvenience, persecution, imprisonment, and martyrdom as *"Christians"* and *"in the will of God."* They have been reproached for the very name of the Christ they have sought to emulate, and in the behalf of God whom they obeyed (1 Pet. 4:14-19).

Ananias of Damascus was instructed to go to the newly converted Saul of Tarsus, and it was explained to the remonstrating disciple, hesitant to embark on this mission, that Saul was a chosen vessel who would yet be shown many things he would suffer for the sake of the Name of the Lord. Because of his pioneer offensive into the spiritual conflict, he encountered suffering (Acts 9:11-16). He could say, *"Satan hindered," "lest Satan should get an advantage,"* and he could speak of being more than a minister of Christ by virtue of the excess of suffering that his service entailed (see 2 Cor. 11:23-28).

Job was brought into a protracted experience of varied and deepening trial, not because of sin or service, but because of the value of his testimony, which, rising to heaven, was maligned by Satan. He insinuated that Job feared God and avoided evil only because it paid him to do so. The testimony of the righteous man could only be preserved in its power by allowing the benefits of his godliness to be removed. *"But in all this Job sinned not, nor charged God with foolishness,"* nor did he *"sin with his lips"* (Job 1:22; 2:10). Thus Satan was silenced and is not mentioned again in the ensuing record. But where Satan finished God began, and refined the character of His servant, eventually repaying him with interest for all that he had lost through the calumny of the adversary.

But the inevitable suffering of the Christian life (1 Pet. 4:1 and 12), whether experienced in the world, the home, or in the Church, because of evil actions, righteous ways, Christian conduct, service, or the Devil's malevolence and vindictiveness, whatever forms it takes, always yields the same blessed result in the character of believers. It will refine the faith, adjust the character, establish, strengthen, and settle the people of God.

Now for a little while, if need be, ye have been put to grief in manifold temptations, that the proof of your faith, being more precious than gold that perisheth though it is proved by fire, might be found unto praise and glory and honor at the revelation of Jesus Christ (1 Pet. 1:6-7).

And the God of all grace, who called you into His eternal glory in Christ, after that ye have suffered a little while, shall Himself perfect, stablish, strengthen you. To Him be the dominion for ever and ever. Amen (1 Pet. 5:10-11).

In the light of the foregoing there is hardly need to expose the evil of the supposition that the misfortunes of believers are punitive; they may be for discipline, instruction, testimony, purification and transformation, fellowship, or for the glory of God.

CHAPTER ELEVEN

The Objectives of Divine Visitation

(1) *To Make Men Conscious of their own Fleeting Existence and of God's Eternal Being:*

The visitations of God though punitive are at the same time educative. One of their objects is to teach men by the lessons of solemn circumstances what might have been learned by easier means. The teachable mind of the humble will learn by happier means the things that the proud and worldly-wise must be made to know by force of visitation. The wonders of nature and the revelations of the Bible teach that God is God, the sovereign and eternal Lord. When this is acknowledged, the gospel can follow, the message that makes known His love revealed in the gift of His Son. But days will come when men refuse to hear the gospel, deny the claims of God, and even His very existence. God has designed that in such days His providence shall operate in a way which will cause these men to recognize Him; and the Maker of men knows well how to teach men His existence and power, even though by painful lessons.

The veracity of Bible teachings regarding God and about sin must be realized by men in spite of the deceptions of earth and all its Babel of doctrines and darkness. It must be brought home to men *that* God is, *who* He is, and that sin against Him is a serious matter. Atheists, infidels, materialists, the indifferent and profligate, have been brought into circumstances in which they have been compelled to confess His existence, often coming into straits that compel them to cry to Him for aid.

Sir Winston Churchill in his book, *My Early Days,* confesses to a phase of violent anti-religious feelings, when he turned to reason and philosophy; but he says quite plainly that the hour of danger exposed these things as fair weather friends, publicly declaring that he was made to cry to God. He also says that, when he escaped from Pretoria, he found himself in circumstances out of which only the help of God could extricate him. Filled with the dread of being recaptured and dragged back to Pretoria, in his extremity he cried to God. He recounts that circumstances turned out so unexpectedly for his deliverance that he could attribute them to none other than the hand of God. In the same way, many who have become indifferent and antagonistic have been made to acknowledge God through the circumstances into which He has brought them.

This illustrates what has taken place in the lives of men of every age in times of danger and need. Portrayed in the 107th Psalm are four classes of people brought by

Providence into four kinds of need: the traveller (vv. 4-6), the rebel (vv. 10-16), the foolish (vv. 17-22) and the mariner (vv. 23-32), who, at an end of themselves and natural resources, cry in their extremity to God who hears them and brings deliverance to each. Observing this, the Psalmist bursts forth with the words, *"Oh, that men would praise the Lord for His goodness and for His wonderful works to the children of men"* (Ps. 107:8, 15, 21, 31). The people of each type, in separate circumstances of difficulty, learned the same lesson of dependence on God for existence and for the means to sustain it.

But such acknowledgment of God, even though it may be intended to lead to it, does not involve conversion. It is something far greater to be brought into a relationship with Him as Father than to recognize Him only as Creator and Lord of providence.

The operations of providence are designed to make men acknowledge God and recognize that they depend on Him. In this way His lower governmental realm serves the higher gospel realm in the same way as the material realm serves them both.

Whereas God is the Creator and Preserver of all (Col. 1:16-17) and Controller of the providences which affect all, He is the Father of only those who have received the Lord Jesus. And it pertains to the gospel alone to bring men to redemption, as the result of which they become the children of God.

The mariners of the psalm just mentioned cried to God as His creatures and proved His deliverance in their circumstances. Whether anything more resulted is to be questioned. There seems to be no evidence in the psalm that they were brought to know God personally. They acknowledged His existence and power and cried because of their extremity. But nothing is said to the effect that they were conscious of spiritual need; no mention is made that it was met; not even a suggestion that they were exercised about it.

Though through these experiences people have been brought to acknowledge God, they may or may not result in salvation. A nation can acknowledge God by having a day of prayer without those who support it being con-verted because they do so. Even so, instances can be mul-tiplied to show that Providence does bring men, women and children to the gospel, through which they are saved.

Evacuation has taken thousands of children from the cities to places where many of them, for the first time, have heard the gospel. Not a few have been converted, and some have in turn been used to bring their parents to the Lord.

Many unconverted and heedless young men, uprooted from the comfort of familiar social circles, in the strange-ness of life in the armed services, faced with danger, have been sobered, and have lent an ear to the Word of God.

Thousands facing death have, as the dying thief, turned to the Lord in repentance. Thousands more in the linger-ing trials of concentration camps have found the Saviour. And many having lost homes have, through Christ, found an eternal Home.

Nevertheless, men like Pharaoh may acknowledge God because of some visitation without coming to know Him as Father. They comply (because they are forced to) with the requirements of the realm of providence, but fall short of compliance with the gospel invitation into the realm of redemption and grace.

Furthermore, the fact that the truth of God has been brought home to them in life will, if they are not saved as the result, leave them without excuse, and add to their condemnation in the coming day, when at the Great White Throne God is vindicated, and the dead, small and great, are judged (Rev. 20:11-15).

The great monarch of Egypt, who said, *"Who is Jehovah that I should hearken unto His voice? I know not Jehovah,"*[1] perished eventually, though he was made to know by visitation at least five things about the character and Being of God. *"In this thou shalt know that I am the LORD"* (Ex. 7:17), so the river was turned to blood, and he was made to know that God was LORD above the Nile-god and the gods of Egypt.

The fixed time for the removal of the scourge of frogs that idolatry was powerless to prevent, showed the supremacy of the LORD: *"that thou mayest know that there is none like unto the LORD our God"* (Ex. 8:10).

The sign of redemption preserving the Israelites from the swarms of flies infesting Egypt not only taught Pharaoh and his people that Israel's God was supreme in heaven, but was *"to the end that ye may know that I am the LORD in the midst of the earth"* (Ex. 8:22).

The boils coming upon the magicians, who wielded the power of idolatry, demonstrated a superior power. The further plagues, as they came upon Pharaoh himself, his

163

servants and his people, showed that no power in Egypt could hold back the visitations of the Lord. Together these happenings were designed that *"thou mayest know that there is none like Me in all the earth"* (Ex. 9:14).

The thunders and hail that came at God's command, ceasing instantaneously that the same command, demonstrated God's proprietorship of earth, being controlled so that Pharaoh might know at the earth is the LORD'S (Ex. 9:28). Thus the object of the visitation was secured, and Pharaoh was made to know: the existence of God; the supremacy of God; the knowledge of God's power in the very land of his own power; the supremacy of God's power in the whole earth—above and in spite of every other power known on earth; finally learning to his further cost that the land he had prized as his own was only leased, the freehold being in the hand of the Creator.

Like Pharaoh, many people who had rarely, if ever, bent their knees in prayer, during nights of bombing, in the midst of earthquakes, or at the deathbed of a loved one, have been made to acknowledge God, often crying to Him in their fear and need.

These mighty governmental interpositions of God are designed to make men aware of Him.[2] As the cherished things of life totter and fall, men fear and are brought face to face with absolute reality, and as the tawdry treasures to which they have clung vanish in the flames, men, stripped of all they hold dear, cry to God. But though this is true, it is often true, too, that like Pharaoh, when there is respite, they turn back to the same follies and sins rather than give heed in the quietness of the respite to the gentler voice of God in the gospel that would lead them to the blessings of eternal life.

(2) *To Teach the Fruitlessness of Sin* (Jer. 2:19):

God also moves in the circumstances of men with the object of making them conscious that sin is of no profit. By evil circumstances following sin and better circumstances issuing from righteousness, on a sort of profit and loss basis, men are made to know the folly of sin and the wisdom of righteousness. There is still a blessing that follows righteousness. But to the sinner there will be travail (Eccl. 2:26). Ill-gotten gain always dissipates itself; the treacherous will always reap treachery; the ruthless will always be overtaken by ruthlessness; they who take the sword in aggression will find it comes back upon them; the covetous, worshipping wealth and amassing it, will find it a curse. Chaining themselves body and soul to the wheels of business, men find themselves slaves in their whirl. The woman founder of an evil cult that taught there was no such thing as disease, died of a loathsome malady. So the mills of God grind, exposing the folly of individuals, nations and states, offering education and instruction to the sons of men, while the cry of wisdom sounds amidst it all, calling men to turn from evil.

(3) *To Correct and Adjust Life:*

God's ways of bringing home to men the reality of His existence and power, and of making men realize that sin does not pay, prove at the same time to be a preservative. This further object becomes evident to us in the words of

Elihu, *"that He may withdraw man from his purpose"* (Job 33:17). Life sometimes becomes inflated—but visitation pricks the bubble and brings men back to the basic facts of their existence, thus preserving proper institutions. This is to be especially seen in times of war, which so dreadfully expose the failures of much-vaunted civilization when the cream of the world's brains is devoted to the destruction of fellow-men in fearful ways. Man professes to go on improving, but the professed improvements of his system are exposed in the days of visitation, when their fruit becomes ripe.

All this seems in measure to carry out the idea expressed in the words of Jeremiah 30:11: *"I will correct thee with judgment."* So the corrective circumstances come into the history of men and nations, to withdraw from folly to the saner existence of following the principles of God and living in His fear.

The objects of the governmental ways of God are thus threefold: to make men know that God is the Lord; to show the folly and result of human sin; and to prove corrective and preservative by bringing things back, in a measure, toward right standards and proper principles of existence.

The ways of God produce these ends for a time; yet it is true, as Zephaniah states, *"that though He bringeth His judgment to light...the unjust knoweth no shame"* (Zeph. 3:5). *"I said, Surely thou wilt fear Me, thou wilt receive instruction...howsoever I punished them; but they rose early and corrupted all their doings"* (Zeph. 3:7). Days of visitation do produce effects, but there is a sense in which their waves fall back in defeat; yet we shall see in later chapters that the tide of God's government ultimately wins.

ENDNOTES:

1. The word LORD is the translation of the grand title JEHOVAH, the meaning and implication of which will repay consideration. It is said to be composed of the verb "to be" in the past, present and future tenses, and implies, "He that ever was," "who always is," "who ever is to come," the eternal, unchanging Being who ever is all that He was and who always will be what He is. His name is "I AM that I AM."

A human being exists for so short a time on earth that if he tried to describe himself in similar language, the terms would be, "I am what I was not," for a short while before he did not exist. The language of man describing himself needs as well to be, "I am what I shall not be," for in so short a while, "Time like an ever rolling stream bears all its sons away." But the divine Being, "I AM," exists independent, unchanging, permanent. So the triune God is described by the title "JEHOVAH," the ETERNAL. Whether we think of the Son who said, *"Before Abraham was I AM,"* or the Spirit, who is called the Eternal Spirit, by whom the words of the Son take shape in creation, or the Father who is indisputably eternal, the title JEHOVAH is a fitting description of the Godhead which is one in substance but three in person. Thus Jehovah Elohim draws from no source, for He is Himself the Source of all, the Beginning, Cause, Creator, and Sustainer of every other form of being, on whom all depend and from whom all draw the means of existence.

Our being is limited and dependent; but when men, forgetting God, behave as though they were independent, God brings about circumstances that demonstrate the innate weakness and dependence of the creature.

167

2. The Book of the prophet Ezekiel will demonstrate that one of the objects of God in visitations is to make men know that He is LORD. No less than sixty-four times, before the end of his thirty-ninth chapter the words occur, *"and they shall know that I am the LORD."* The following quotation is an example:

> *Thus saith the Lord GOD: Behold I am against thee, O Zidon; and I will be glorified in the midst of thee: and they shall know that I am the LORD, when I shall have executed judgments in her, and shall be sanctified in her. For I will send into her pestilence and blood in her streets; and the wounded shall fall in the midst of her, with the sword upon her on every side; and they shall know that I am the LORD* (Ezek. 28:22-23).

Exodus, Ezekiel, the prophets, the Psalms, and all the ways of God, show it to be imperative that men be made to know that God is eternal and independent, while they are small, thoroughly dependent creatures of time.

CHAPTER TWELVE

The Temporal Blessings of God

Isaiah speaks of *"well"* for the righteous and of *"woe"* for the wicked, as he addresses them both in the following words:

> Woe unto their soul! for they have rewarded evil unto themselves! Say ye of the righteous, that it shall be well with him; for they shall eat the fruit of their doings. Woe unto the wicked! it shall be ill with him: for the reward of his hands shall be given him (Isa. 3:9-11).

We have already seen that circumstances are the fruit of men's doings and that men, by behavior which culminates in visitation, can reward themselves evil. In the opposite way others eat the better fruit of better doings. The circumstances that follow in the wake of each are as much in contrast as the behavior of the two kinds of people. So the temporal blessings of God on those that recognize Him stand out in contrast to His visitations for the evil of others.

Whenever it can be consistent with His principles, God will allow His temporal blessings. In lovingkindness He gives fertility and full harvest rather than drought, barrenness and famine; congenial behavior of the elements instead of adverse storms; freedom from pests that devour the crops produced by the earth. He blesses and gives health and length of days to men instead of sickness, plague and untimely death; wholesome occupation and work rather than languishing idleness enforced by visitation; confidence and quiet security in place of fret and fear of evil; freedom from oppression, despotism and vassalage to the state; raised national status rather than depravity; elevation rather than decline, and increase rather than diminution.

Righteous rule, just judgment, prosperity and peace also are blessings which proceed from Him and are the result of the hand of God. No amount of human ingenuity or effort can produce them artificially in the experience of men; they come only as the result of the working of divine principles and are withdrawn by the same principles. The laws that govern these circumstances are as relentless as gravity, though more complex to understand.

All these mercies, enumerated in contrast to the evils of visitation, are the issue of moral laws, the result of divine principles.

Disregarding these principles, the world may unite itself to effect peace and apply its ingenuity to bring about prosperity, but the peace and prosperity, visualized and sought, will prove a mirage, eluding its seekers. *"There is no peace...unto the wicked"* (Isa. 48:22), nor

170

lasting prosperity for the ungodly, however great their efforts or ingenuity be in the pursuit of the good they desire.

The good things of God that are enjoyed in the circumstances of men and nations come from the hand of God alone, and are consequent upon moral conditions.

If these good things were unwisely allowed and indiscriminately scattered they would result in ultimate ill. A sharp knife is useful and can be a blessing, but it forms no part of an infant's possessions for the simple reason that the infant has not the ability to use it rightly. So the mercies of peace and prosperity are denied men when they lack the conditions that are required and the fitness that is demanded. The possession and right use of the things most valued in life follow fitness and worth. When these conditions are fulfilled by the individual or the nation, the mercies of God will be enjoyed.

In the Christian dispensation long life and well-being in good circumstances are promised to the obedient child in the words of Ephesians 6:2-3, *"Honor thy father and mother that it may be well with thee and thou mayest live long on the earth"* (1 Tim. 4:8, 10; Titus 3:8; Lk. 18:29-30 may be referred to in this connection.)

This is in keeping with the key phrase, *"that it may be well with thee,"* found in the Old Testament more times than can be easily recounted, promising good, well-being and long life to those wise enough to submit to the ways of God. Most of the passages which speak of the temporal blessings of God relate to the nation of Israel, but while that is true, it is also true that these and many other scriptures contain principles that apply in general. It holds good without respect to persons or time that *"it shall be well with them that fear God"* (Eccl. 8:12). Cornelius is an example, though he needed to be saved. His good moral life was rewarded by the good circumstances which he enjoyed. In the same way, *"Righteousness exalteth a nation, but sin is a reproach to any people"* (Prov. 14:34), and *"By the blessing of the upright the city is exalted, but it is overthrown by the mouth of the wicked"* (Prov. 11:11).

Israel was promised that it would be well with them if they did what was upright and good (Deut. 6:3, 18), executed civil justice (Deut. 19:13) and religious honesty (Deut. 4:40). If so, the nation should increase in numbers and prosper in a congenial land full of the riches of nature. Immunity from envy and attack was to be theirs if they diligently walked in the fear of God. *"I will...enlarge thy borders, neither shall any man desire thy land"* (Ex. 34:24), were the words that contain a principle that holds good for any nation at any time.

God's desire to grant temporal blessing, as well as the principles upon which those blessings come, are expressed in the words,

> *O that there was such an heart in them that they would fear Me, and keep all My commandments always, that it might be well with them and with their children for ever* (Deut. 5:29).

The idea of our chapter is summed up in the truth found in Jeremiah 22:13-19, that contrast the experiences of Josiah and Eliakim, or Jehoiakim (as Pharaoh Necho renamed him, 2 Ki. 23:34). Josiah, the father, had reigned over Judah in God-fearing equity for thirty-one years, but his son, Jehoiakim, was ignominiously dismissed from power after eleven years. The godly father from his youth had put down superstition and immorality, removed idolatry, publicly owned God and obeyed His laws, in faithfulness doing justice and judgment in deciding the cause of the poor and needy.

His covetous son, oblivious to the principle that *"the prince...that hateth covetousness shall prolong his days"* (Prov. 28:16), thought security was assured by self-seeking, possession, and force. Both father and son reaped the two kinds of fruit from their respective doings. Of Josiah it is said that *"it was well with him."* But the woes of God were pronounced on the selfish, avaricious Jehoiakim and were fulfilled in the visitations which followed: his reign was reduced to comparatively few years, and death, ignominious and unmourned, was the sad end of the evil king. The contrast is sharp and distinct. Josiah was honored and blessed in fulfillment of the abiding principle, *"them that honor Me I will honor, and they that despise Me shall be lightly esteemed"* (1 Sam. 2:30).

The temporal blessings of God will flow and be enjoyed in the circumstances of this life until men, taking them for granted, become unthankful, and in their unthankfulness undervalue the principles by which these blessings come, forgetting and even despising the God who gives them. Therefore He righteously *"withholds the good things"* (Jer. 5:25), replacing them by the sad circumstances of visitation. In turn, the evil circumstances have their salutary effect, chastening and, in measure, humbling men; the purposes of God are fulfilled, and in mercy He restores temporal blessing after the clouds of visitation.

Whether we consider the visitations of God or His temporal blessings, the fact of a nation's responsibility to God is emphasized. It is impossible to evade or side-track the cycle of His laws. Sin will bring sorrow, the fear of God will bring benefit. If plans are made and policies formed without regard to God's principles, whatever be the power or cleverness, or whatever the seeming success for the moment, those plans will miscarry and the structures raised will come crashing to the ground.

As in further chapters we look at the prophecies of Christ concerning the end of this age, it will become clear that the greater efforts of men to secure peace and prosperity for themselves apart from Bible principle, will be but the forerulers of greater sorrows and more violent calamities. But as men are bowed before God in sincerity and turn to the Word of God in a childlike spirit, renouncing their headiness and worldly wisdom, they will learn the fear of God which is the beginning of wisdom and will reap the good of such wisdom.

CHAPTER THIRTEEN

The Purposes of God

The system of moral government does not express all that is in the mind of God. In fact it is only a system to maintain a measure of order during the time in which greater purposes are being carried out. Moral government affects circumstances which are outward and passing. But God has purposes which operate within, the accomplishments of which are eternal and abiding.

ONE COMPREHENSIVE PURPOSE, THE GOAL OF THE AGES

All these purposes of God concentrate on one transcending purpose, the establishment of the perfect kingdom of the new heavens and the new earth. This purpose is portrayed as complete in the last vision of the Bible, which depicts the nations in a state of ordered blessing and joy, God dwelling with them and reigning over them from the midst of the Golden City. The Throne of God and the Lamb constitutes that city's sanctuary, from which the river of blessing flows, and through its broad highway the glory and praise of the nations is brought to God. The glory of God shines from the Lamb, and, mirrored and diffused by the city and its transparent, gem-studded walls, becomes the light of the new earth in which the nations walk. Those with washed robes partake of the fruitful Tree of Life and, in the energy derived from it, His servants serve Him and, seeing His face, reflect His character throughout the ages of ages.

All the governments of God from the foundation of the world contribute to this end. Creation, by bringing into existence and controlling the universe, provides a platform on which Providence arranges the relationships and controls the experiences of mankind. Redemption, working in the midst of all, accomplishes the spiritual work of God in individual hearts, and produces those who form part of the people who will enjoy the blessings of the new heavens and the new earth. All the ages, like the work days of God's first creation, work toward the final rest of God. Each succeeding age, like the six days of the old creation, accomplishes a purpose, and yields a piece of different character. In this new creation, the masterpiece of God, all the families in heaven and earth will be to His glory through Christ Jesus (Eph. 3:15, 21).

THE SUBSIDIARY PURPOSES

Though in the words of the vision it is said that the Lord God Almighty and the Lamb are the temple of the city, the whole scene is described as the *"tabernacle* (the tent) *of God is with men."* In the ordinary use of language a tabernacle or tent indicates something less permanent than a temple. But that this less permanent idea is not conveyed is evident from the plain statement that it continues for ever and ever. The choice of the word *"tabernacle"* is deliberate, and used to convey the association of ideas between Israel's ancient tabernacle and the new heavens and the new earth. Israel's tabernacle, situated in the midst of the priesthood, the Levites and the tribes, was the dwelling place of God and the throne of the theocracy. Here is a picture of the completed purposes of God—the tabernacle of God with men, the everlasting theocracy of the new heavens and the new earth.

When this purpose is realized, God will dwell in the midst of several circles of the redeemed. From the farthest circumference men will draw near to God, each according to his privilege and capacity, bringing to Him their glory and honor, and going forth with His benediction upon them.

The three kinds of people around Israel's symbolic tabernacle illustrate the three classes of the redeemed. First there is the Church, corresponding to the priesthood which encamped immediately around the dwelling place of God. The Jews are illustrated by the Levites who formed a second circle, and the nations are represented by the tribes which encamped outside of and around these in a third circle. Within each circle of the redeemed there will, no doubt, be different ranks and positions such as are suggested by the heads of families, elders and princes.

A consideration of the companies of the redeemed enumerated in a later chapter will prove suggestive to the thoughtful reader. However, the short passage set out below speaks of these three groups of the redeemed in the order in which they are formed.

The Church:

God at the first did visit the Gentiles to take out of them a people for His name (Acts 15:14).

Israel:

After this I will return and will build again the tabernacle of David which is fallen down and I will build again the ruins thereof and I will set it up (Acts 15:16).

The Gentile nations:

That the residue of men might seek after the Lord and all the Gentiles upon whom My name is called, saith the Lord, who doeth all these things (Acts 15:17).

The expression, *"after these things,"* indicates that the restoration of the royal house of David and the development of national purposes for the Jews await the completion of the work commenced at Pentecost, and described as, *"God visiting the Gentiles to take out of them a people for His name."* Other scriptures describe it as the *"Church,"* and show it to be the purpose of God peculiar to the present age, which concludes at the coming of Christ. Then the purpose for Israel will materialize and finally the purposes for the nations take shape. It is impossible for the nations to enjoy their blessing until Israel is restored and it is equally impossible for Israel to be restored until the Church is complete.

In the chapter on "The Destiny of Nations," it is shown that, consequent to the Second Advent of the Lord Jesus, the nations will occupy their own lands and rejoice in the Eden blessings of the reign of Christ. Reflecting His glory in their various types, they will be absorbed in His obedience and pleasure. Here we need only show a little of God's purpose for Israel and then devote our attention to the present purpose of God.

ISRAEL

(1) *The Divine Purpose for them:*

The purpose of God for Israel is described in the words of God to their leader soon after their exodus from Egypt:

Ye shall be a peculiar treasure unto Me from above all people: for all the earth is Mine: and ye shall be unto Me a kingdom of priests and an holy nation (Ex. 19:5-6).

It is a royal and sacred position, and a holy character was to make them His jewels (Mal. 3:17). Thus fitted, they were intended to stand as priest between God and the other nations, being the channel of His blessing to them.

(2) *Their History and Failure:*

The inspired history of this nation is one of tremendous privileges and of awful failure. Even as God was speaking to Moses in the mount, the people were bowing to the Egyptian idol in the plain. Through sin and unfaithfulness the wonderful covenant was broken, and that which was designed for their blessing became their curse.

Called to be a nation of priests, they became a nation of merchants. Brought out from Egypt's slavery to separation and sanctification, they became involved in the sins of the other nations and lost their distinctive character and position. The purpose of God was missed, being based as it was on a covenant of law, under which the blessing depended on the obedience of the people. But what failed under law will be realized under grace; for the New Covenant, which is instituted through the mediatorship of Christ and based on His sacrifice, will, in a coming day, cause the full glory and blessings of the original purpose to be enjoyed under the Melchizedek Priesthood of Christ.

(3) *Their Rejection and Blindness:*

Israel's great sin of the rejection of Christ was followed by their rejection of the gospel and by concerted attempts to frustrate its purposes of blessing to others (1 Thess. 2:14-16). For this reason God (as Rom. 11 shows) has set them as a nation aside during this age. Six things are said which describe their present position in the purposes of God:

a. They stumbled (v. 11)
b. Their fall (v. 12)
c Their casting away (v. 15)
d. They are broken off (v. 17)
e. They are under severity (v. 22)
f. They are subject to blindness (v. 25)

Thus has God suspended their special privileges, and

under His providential judgments, scattered them, until He has completed the work of taking out of the nations the unique company of which we go on to speak. At present the Jewish nation is under the severity of God, their branches are broken off from the trunk of His blessings, and a judicial blindness has settled upon the hearts of the people once so favored of God.

The problem of the Jew is a burdensome stone to the nations (Zech. 12:3) and will not be solved until God in His own time returns to bless them; they are like the copestone of a pyramid, which fits nowhere but at the top, and until they are the head of the nations through sovereign grace they will be the problem of the nations.

(4) *Their Future Salvation and Glory:*

The restoration of Israel is predicted in terms as distinct and clear as those used to describe their present alienation from the ways of God. Five things are said of their future and will be true of them when the *"fullness of the Gentiles is come in"* (Rom. 11:25):

1. Their fullness (v. 12)
2. Their receiving again (v. 15)
3. Their grafting in again (v. 23)
4. They will be saved (v. 26)
5. They will have sins taken away (v. 27)

Then their destiny will be realized and the following description be true of them:

And they shall build the old wastes, they shall raise up the former desolations, and they shall repair the waste

181

cities, the desolations of many generations. And strangers shall stand and feed your flocks, and aliens shall be your plowmen and your vinedressers. But ye shall be named the priests of the Lord: men shall call you the ministers of our God: ye shall eat the wealth of the nations, and in their glory shall ye boast yourselves (Isa. 61:4-6).

Thou shalt also be a crown of beauty in the hand of the Lord, and a royal diadem in the hand of thy God. Thou shalt no more be termed Forsaken; neither shall thy land any more be termed Desolate: but thou shalt be called Hephzibah, and thy land Beulah; for the Lord delighteth in thee, and thy land shall be married (Isa. 62:3-4).

(5) *The Present Purpose:*

It is not the purpose of God to convert the world, nor to bring about, in this age, the material kingdom of God on earth. That belongs to the coming age, which cannot begin without the personal return of the rejected Lord Jesus. God, in reciprocal righteousness, has rejected the present constitution of the world, because of the world's rejection of Christ (Jn. 12:31-32), but in mercy He allows it to continue on during this age, while He acts in grace through the gospel, and builds the *Ekklesia* of individuals who receive its message, with a view to instituting a new world.

Since the rejection and crucifixion of Christ, there is no word in the Scriptures to support the idea of a material kingdom of God on earth in the present age. Had it been God's purpose to set up a kingdom of material blessings the twenty centuries of the present age would proclaim its failure, and the present century with its awful wars and barbarism would declare the inability of God to carry out that purpose. The ever-recurring outbreaks of evil expose the folly of thinking it is God's object to establish the kingdom in this age.

The purpose of each succeeding age differs as much as did the work of each day of creation. To suppose that God was endeavoring to make man on the fifth day, when the sea monsters were the result, would be the greatest folly, and what is more, an insult to God. It is no less a folly and not less an insult to suppose that God is at present endeavoring to do the work of the next age, that of setting up a kingdom of peace and blessing. The present purpose is not to bless a world of nations as nations with the blessings of redemption, which will involve setting up permanently the glorious kingdom in their midst. Neither is it the purpose of the present age to bless the Jew as a nation, nor yet to realize the glory that has been promised to him.

Although Providence, on the principles that we have seen from the Scriptures, controls the circumstances of Jewish and Gentile nations according to their behavior, it is only to make their ordered existence possible for a time during which redemption carries out the work of forming a unique company. Having completed this spiritual work and removed this company from earth, God will, in the short term at the end of the age, swiftly and irresistibly act to reinstate the Jew, deal exhaustively with sin among the Gentile nations and bring in the kingdom on earth.

This company of people which through the gospel is being formed in this age, and for the completion of which all other purposes wait (see Rom. 8:19), is described in the following list:

a. A people for His Name (Acts 15:14).
b. A company given to Christ out of the world (Jn. 17:6, 11, 14, 16).
c A body of which Christ is Head (Eph. 1:22-23; 1 Cor. 12:12-13)
d. A sacred building (Eph. 2:20-23).
e. A brotherhood in the midst of the world (1 Pet. 2:17; 5:9).
f. A family fellowship of light, life, and love (1 Jn. 1:3-5)
g. A bridal company espoused to Christ Himself (Eph. 5:31-32; 2 Cor. 11:2).

Each of these terms forbids the idea of a present set of social or material conditions for the nations and supports the concept of a distinct body of unique character. It will be observed that the above list has been taken from the words of Christ, the early apostolic council, and the teachings of Peter, Paul and John, and thus presents the idea of the New Testament *in toto*.

This company was designated the *Ekklesia* by the Lord Jesus and was first spoken of in the second part of the Gospel by Matthew (16:18). In this Gospel there is an important change in character noticeable, as the reader passes from chapter 12 to chapter 13. Prior to the end of chapter 12, there are no parables, but after it Christ rarely taught without one. The record begins with the genealogy from the royal line and continues by presenting Christ as the King, showing that He was born a King and worshiped as such. We find Him preaching the principles of His kingdom and performing the ten public miracles which establish His credentials as the divine Messiah and heaven-sent King.

But after His rejection by the leaders of the people (9:34; 12:14), His mode of public address was changed and the parable form of teaching adopted (see ch. 13). By this new mode of teaching a phase of the kingdom "in mystery" or "in secret" was outlined, in contrast to an outward and apparent form of the kingdom in glory. Later He explained that during this secret phase, which takes place prior to the realization of the kingdom in its unveiled glory at the second Advent of Christ (Mt. 24:30-31), He would build His *Ekklesia* (Mt. 16:18).

The term *Ekklesia,* the title of this company of people, requires consideration, especially as it cannot adequately be translated by any word in current English. It occurs no less than 118 times in the New Testament and in our Authorized Version is translated "Church" 115 times and "assembly" three times. It means to "summon forth" or "call out of" and is formed from two words, one of which means "out of" and the other "to call." For a people to bear this title involves first the idea of their being called, then of their response to that call, and finally, of a new relationship with one another which results in the formation of a company distinct from previous associations.

185

This calling out and calling together is the work of the present age; God is now using the message of *"Christ, and Him crucified,"* to summon forth individuals, who, upon conversion, are incorporated into this unique company. It is clearly taught that God will not bid creation cease its groan through the setting up of His kingdom of blessing and peace until after this company is completed and glorified in heaven (Rom. 8:19-21).

There will be no radical changes in earth, nor in the constitution of the world, until this company is completed. Providence will continue to operate and the mercies of God will be known in circumstances, but only in a way which is tributary to the gospel of His grace that proclaims salvation in Christ Jesus for the individual.

God's first worldwide intervention that will fundamentally change all the affairs of this earth will be the removal of His completed Church. Then the Lord Jesus Himself *"will descend from heaven with a shout, with the voice of the archangel, and the trump of God." "In a moment, in the twinkling of an eye,"* the whole Church will be translated to His presence, where she will realize the glory for which she was destined from before the foundation of the world.

This great event, commencing the *parousia* of Christ, will set in motion the happenings of the end of the age with its intensified and accelerated visitations, and lead up to the manifestation of the Lord Jesus as the King of kings and Lord of lords, with the consequent dawn of the long awaited kingdom of blessing and peace for the nations.

Until then, those who have already entered the kingdom of God by faith in Christ, and who await the time when God will realize His purposes, have a ministry to execute on behalf of a groaning creation. In this way the lot of men may be eased, and the purposes of God hastened. This ministry is the subject of a later chapter, which aims to show the high dignity to which the Christian is called, and the great measure in which, without actual intervention, that ministry may be effective in human blessing.

CHAPTER FOURTEEN

The Kingdom of God

We read of the kingdom of God many times in the New Testament, and although the expression in its exact form is not present in the Old Testament, the idea permeates the whole of those scriptures. Obadiah in his closing verse looks forward to a day which the kingdom shall be the Lord's, and Daniel foretells a time when the God of heaven—who now rules providentially setting up and putting down kings (Dan. 4:1-17, 25-26)—will set up an actual kingdom on earth. Its constitution will be perfect and therefore everlasting and the people of it, not being removed by death and replaced by new generations as people are now, will remain unchanged in its abiding blessing (Dan. 2:44). From days as far back as Enoch it has been the hope of every true believer that God would expunge evil from the earth, and that He Himself take the reins, directly administering earth's affairs.

In this subject, as in all other matters of revelation, there is a progress of doctrine throughout the pages of the Bible. At the close of the Book of Revelation the doctrine of the kingdom of God finds its full development in the vision of the new heaven and new earth, in which God will tabernacle with men again by means of the Holy

City. When this kingdom of heaven and earth is realized, no sorrow, pain, defilement, or death shall mar the scene, and men, perfected, under the blessed control of God and the Lamb, will know the constant refreshing of the river of life and the perpetual sustenance of the tree of life. In virtue of this fullness of the Spirit and enjoyment of Christ, sacred service to God will occupy their happy days, the sunshine of which will never be dimmed.

The simplest reader discerns the fact of the kingdom and a child can enjoy the prospect of the above vision. Yet no rapt seer, privileged apostle, or serious Bible student can unravel all the meaning of each stage of the development of the teaching regarding the kingdom. But though it is true in this study, as in all other studies, that if any-one thinks he knows anything, he knows nothing as he ought to know it (1 Cor. 8:2), yet there are things revealed so clearly that a child can grasp them.

We shall be helped to form balanced and proportioned ideas by observing some of the corrections made by the Lord Jesus. He was often at issue with the Pharisees on points of doctrine and what He thus taught them at these times is recorded to teach us.

Probably consequent on His preaching about the king-dom, there was an occasion when they demanded of Him to know when the kingdom of God should come. It is evi-dent that their ideas of the kingdom were limited to a set of conditions and circumstances—a material kingdom. The Lord's answer emphasized the antithesis to this, and the idea He expressed was at the extreme other end of the swing of the pendulum. He said,

The kingdom of God cometh not with outward show...for behold the kingdom of God is within you (Lk. 17:20-21).

Their thoughts were not in opposition to the teaching of the Old Testament, for it was from there that they derived them. But what the Lord wished to correct was this: that the kingdom of God does not consist only in a set of conditions and a material environment and constitution by which the world is prepared for man. It consists also in a set of conditions *within* man, by means of which individuals are prepared for that world.

Therefore the first great development in teaching on the kingdom as we come to the Gospels is this—that men as individuals need to be as much prepared within themselves as the world needs to be prepared around them. The blight of sin and the effects of the Fall are seen around us in creation and circumstances, but they are also to be seen in every individual, polluting the very springs of his being.

The Pharisees were not alone in their limited idea of a material kingdom, for, according to Mark 11:10, the multitude who hailed Jesus on His entry into Jerusalem thought only of the kingdom of David, and the minds of the apostles (Acts 1:6) were also dominated by the expectation of the restoration of the kingdom to Israel. The expanded and larger view of the kingdom which is developed in the New Testament embraces all that was expected of a literal material Jewish kingdom on earth but contains spiritual, moral and heavenly features as well.

The thoughtful Nicodemus, not easily swayed like the multitude, nor refusing to be moved like many of the other Pharisees, came to Jesus by night, evidently with a number of questions. In the presence of the Lord his words failed, and the pause after the unfinished oration was used to go right to the heart of the man and to show Nicodemus, who was well instructed, the Old Testament, revelations of a material kingdom, an angle of truth of which he had been altogether ignorant.

The words to the great Teacher of Israel were,

Verily, verily, I say unto you, except a man be born again he cannot see the kingdom of God.

A new kind of birth is required to fit the individual man himself, as apart from this not only would he not be in the kingdom, but would be unable even to visualize it.

Throughout John's 21 chapters almost 80 times the word *world* is used and used in a sense which describes an order of things here on earth in contrast to that order of things out of which the Lord Jesus descended to earth. John the Baptist spoke of Christ as He that cometh from above; and in this way the Lord Jesus uses the term to Nicodemus, *"Ye must be born from above."* Even to visualize, much more to enter, a man needs to pass through the experience of this new and heavenly birth.

In the following words of the Lord, this idea of a birth to fit the individual for the kingdom is expanded, and the Lord Jesus speaks of being *"born of water and of the Spirit,"* of a new genesis produced out of the element of cleansing, and spiritual in character: a new genesis obviously in contrast to anything material or of the senses; not new works but a new man to do them, not a change in doing, but a change in the man. What a bombshell this was to the learned and pious theologian of that day might be discerned by his words, *"How can these things be?"* containing as they do a note of helplessness and despair!

Thus the man who had read of the kingdom, lived for the kingdom, and preached about the kingdom, came to realize that it was a spiritual thing as well as material, and that he would need a power outside of himself to bring him to this spiritual birth before he could visualize its character or enter into its blessing. It was brought home to him that this birth does not take place *"of blood,"* through human lineage; *"nor of the of the flesh,"* by the effort of nature; *"nor of man,"* for it is a thing of super-human origin—*"of God."* Only He can translate men into the kingdom of the Son of His love (Col. 1:13).

So in our thoughts of the kingdom of God, while seeing that the prospect of a material order of blessing is real, we see also that those who will enjoy it will be those who have been fitted for it by a new spiritual birth; being born of God, they will become children of God, and will in that sense be fitted for the kingdom of God.

It is interesting and most instructive to note that the Lord Jesus said nothing to Nicodemus about faith nor about Himself until after the question that indicated his extremity. When brought to an end of himself he said, *"How can these things be?"* the Lord began to tell him of the Son of Man being lifted up, so that those who believe in Him might have everlasting life.

193

In this way the Lord, His apostles, and the whole line of faithful witnesses to this day teach that the first need of man is not the preparation of the kingdom for him, but the preparation—in this individual and spiritual way—of *man himself* for the kingdom.

As we proceed further in the New Testament, it becomes clear that two other kinds of fitness are required for the kingdom of God: fitness of character and fitness of body. A list of negatives, found in 1 Corinthians 6:9-10, and Galatians 5:19-21, excludes from all hope of the kingdom the moral classes described in these verses, and which emphasizes the necessity of moral suitability. It is obvious that life can only follow birth, and that the new life can only follow the new birth. We have just reasons to doubt that a spiritual birth has taken place unless it has been followed by the evidence of spiritual life.

The experience of moral preparation for the kingdom is dual: in the world those who are born of God will find that it is through much tribulation that they are to enter the kingdom (Acts 14) while in their souls it is a matter of righteousness, peace, and joy in the Holy Ghost (Rom. 14:17). The very tribulations that the believer must pass through, be they small or large, will only serve the purpose of preparation for that kingdom.

The kingdom of God, therefore, is first spiritual and operates now in the individual; it is secondly moral, and is produced here and now in the path of obedience and tribulation; finally it is material, and into its real blessings the prepared will be brought, to enjoy eternally the realm which will be prepared for them.

One more strong negative should be considered to give us balanced views and will serve to show that the kingdom in its fullness cannot dawn without the personal return of the Lord Jesus. It is stated in 1 Corinthians 15:50 that flesh and blood cannot inherit the kingdom of God and that therefore a changed body is required for that scene of blessing. When this has taken place, the redeemed will thus have been prepared—spirit, soul and body—to inherit that kingdom. The first possible occasion at which bodies of believers will be changed be when the Lord Himself shall descend from heaven with a shout with the voice of the Archangel and the trump of God (1 Thess. 4:16-17). This great event, as we have seen, will inaugurate the *parousia* and the end of the age, which, leading up to the appearing, will result in the kingdom in all its material blessings.

The Lord Jesus, when before Pontius Pilate, witnessed a good confession (according to 1 Tim. 6:13), in the light of which Timothy himself is charged to flee the things of present material gain (vv. 5-10), and to follow the things of moral good (vv. 11-12). A consideration of all that is recorded of what took place before Pilate will make it evident to the attentive reader that Christ's good confession was made in the words of John 18:36, *"My kingdom is not of this world."*

The kingdom of God is therefore not something produced by the world, not out of the world, nor is it something that the world is developed into, but is in contrast to, and of an entirely different order from, anything that belongs to present systems. Operating now in the individual heart, it can be realized in the world only at the Advent of Christ Himself. So the believer is encouraged to wait for the kingdom, pray for the kingdom, and preach for the kingdom, but never to endeavor to set up the kingdom.

There are two expressions which are paradoxical, but which yield a closing point for our instruction. Daniel speaks very plainly of a kingdom *under* the whole heaven (Dan. 7:27), whereas Paul differentiates, speaking of *"His kingdom, **the heavenly one**"* (2 Tim. 4:18). That there is a commonwealth existing in the heavens is stated in Philippians 3:20, and it seems that it is to this that Paul refers in his last written epistle. That there will be a commonwealth on the earth is equally evident, and to this Daniel refers when he interprets the vision of the Son of Man. The Old Testament saw only the earthly one. The New Testament supports this view, but shows as well a great polity in the heavens which will direct the affairs of the nations on earth. Thus the later revelations make it clear that the kingdom of God is a kingdom of heaven *and* earth with the various orders of redeemed, all born again, all fitted in character and body to fill those places in the various ranks and services of a universal administration of holiness and peace. These orders of the redeemed will have been saved out of different generations and ages to form part of the different companies enumerated elsewhere and to fill different positions in the glad day when the sovereignty of the world is in the hands of our Lord and of His Christ.

CHAPTER FIFTEEN

The Church and Human Circumstances

THE INADEQUACY OF CHRISTIAN ETHICS

The line of demarcation between the world and the Church was more distinct in the first century than today. Then the Church and the Empire were separate. But now many organizations which claim to be Christian, feeling a responsibility to deal with social problems, have become interested in, and in some cases associated with, politics, in the hope of eliminating war and other social evils. At the same time the outward lives of many people have been affected by Christian principles without any inward change of heart toward God. These, approving of righteousness and the finer graces of Christian behavior, emulate what little they can of them, and endeavor to apply their imperfectly conceived ideas of Christianity to politics and government, having as their object the introduction of a moral and social order of righteousness and peace. But all this leaves the real need untouched.

If the so-called Christian organizations and the idealists of the world combined in the application of Christian ethics to the world and its governments, and, as a result, succeeded in eliminating social evils and moral ills, the greatest need of man would still remain. The outside of the cup and of the platter thus cleansed, would leave the inherent sin of human nature as existent as ever (as with the Pharisees of old, see Mt. 23:25-28). Hence, if it were possible, by these means, to remodel the world socially and morally, it would amount only to healing the out-breaks on the skin, and would leave the disease in the system untouched.

Furthermore, though it might make the world more pleasant, it would make it more deceiving, for its very improvements would better conceal the real need, that of the heart before God. Thus, by concealing the vital need, it would contribute to the work of the adversary rather than to the work of God. The success of these efforts would make life a greater mirage, superficially ordered and outwardly apparently healthy, but men, inwardly unchanged and not *"born again,"* would still be estranged from God.

After all, the very evils of the world are a kind of bless-ing, for the existence of these evils emphasizes the reali-ty to which most close their eyes—that things are not right, and that this is so because *men are not right* in heart with God. It is easy to see the social advantages which would result from universal application of the ethics of Christ. Nevertheless, the application of these principles to the world, without individual reception of Christ as personal Saviour and Lord, amounts to seeking the bless-ings before the Blesser, the kingdom conditions before the King, and salvation's results before the reception of the Saviour. When the facts of these efforts are brought out into the light and considered, they reveal the efforts to be, not only misguided (though well-meaning by those who make them) but a refined and cunningly camou-flaged rejection of Christ Himself.

The fall of man through sin against God brought in sorrow and death, but sorrow and death mercifully imposed by God until full redemption should be provid-ed in God's time by the divine emancipator, the Lord Jesus Christ. But soon efforts were made by the line of Cain, who had already rejected the promise of Christ, to make the best of the world without God. The result was the Cainite civilization, which boasted its refinements and improvements, as have the other civilizations which have followed at intervals during the centuries down to that of our time. All these civilizations borrow that which it is possible to borrow of the things of God, and, without regard for the revealed will of God, or the great spiritual need of men's hearts before God, apply that which they borrow to material and social circumstances.

This has always had the same result—further departure from God and consequently multiplied sin, which has ended in chaos, disaster, and divine judgment. In the same way, a modern civilization which uses Christian ethics to make the best of the world without Christ will result in disaster at the end of this age. (Details of this and evidence of it from scripture prophecy are provided in the later chapter on "The End of the Age.") Man's real need is of Christ, not the teachings of Christ, not the ethics of

Christ. His need is *The Christ* as a Person, and as a Person who is Saviour because of His sacrifice and atonement for men.

It follows, therefore, that the work of the Church is not essentially a moral work, nor a social work, but a spiritual one, a work which goes to the root of man's need with a message that presents Christ as a living Saviour and Lord to be personally received. The power of this message of the gospel has millions of times met the need of earth's most wretched sinners and reconciled them to God; and they have gone on to live changed lives which demonstrate that correct morals and proper social behavior are the *fruit* of the heart's being right with God.

The application of Christianity to social and moral needs without individual conversion is not only subversive of the gospel but is impracticable, because of the corruption of the human heart. The lower standards of common morals and basic righteousness are so rarely attained that the attempt to apply the very much higher standards of Christianity is folly.[1]

It is easy to see the social advantages which would result if the ethics of Christ could be universally applied. Many, seeing this as a wondrous dream, try to attain for themselves and the world the present social benefits of these ethics. But let the warning be sounded, for the world is deceived and the professing Church aids in that deception. The teachings of Christ will never work in the world, and, if applied, will end in disaster to individuals, communities, and nations. The full application of the ethics of Christ in the present world would lead only to an end equivalent to Calvary—the execution of Israel's Messiah by the only people in the world with a God-given religion.

The teachings of Christ are not for the world. They were never given to the world nor intended for the world. They are for those alone who have had the experience of conviction and confession of sin followed by that definite, decisive receiving of Christ Himself as a living Saviour and Lord. To take these teachings and apply them to the world, a sphere for which they were never designed, is folly; and, what is far worse, to take them from where they belong without authority is theft.

THE NECESSITY OF JUDGMENT

That there are three spheres of government—material, moral and spiritual—in which three kinds of principles operate, has been shown in an earlier chapter. As a part of His moral government, God has delegated to kings and magistrates authority to punish crime, and to deal by force with the moral and social evils that are found within their jurisdiction. It is also part of His moral government to move one nation against another, to inflict chastisement. Thus, as has been shown, war and other evils are divine visitations. But all this belongs to the realm of providence and moral government, a realm in which it is unfortunately necessary, because of the lawless instincts of men, for force to operate and judgment take place.

Were it not for the force behind the uniformed policeman he would be a laughing-stock; but the fear of an enforced penalty generally commands respect. By means of magistracy and visitations, earth's evils, which would otherwise increase enormously, though never eliminated, are restrained. But these necessary means, though righteous and instituted of God, are not Christian, as is evident from the fact of their existence before the revelation of Christ and those principles peculiar to His people. Their operation prior to the inception of the Church shows that a Church is not necessary for their operation. Whereas instructions are found directing the churches to submit to these institutions, none are found directing the churches to operate or act in these institutions.

The work of the churches is neither moral nor social, still less is it physical and retributive. Though there is a realm, righteously instituted, in which force operates, and in which judgment must be meted out, and though the believer is to be subject to it (and may even suffer righteously or unrighteously in it—see Appendix: "The Suffering of Believers"), he is never called upon to act in the capacity of it.

It seems, in the light of that which in previous chapters has been discovered from the Scriptures, that war must be regarded as one of the necessities of the governmental sphere—at least as long as the nature of man remains unchanged. Nevertheless, though it may in this sense be a necessary part of the moral government of the world, and though in some instances it may appear to be justly waged, it is never Christian. The principle of "an eye for an eye and a tooth for a tooth" applies to the realm of government, but the principle of love applies to those already in the kingdom of God.

A few questions may serve to clarify the implications of all this.

If apparently evil rulers need to be judged, and if God has said, *"Vengeance is Mine; I will repay"* (Rom. 12:19), is it not presumption for the Christian to act?

If God, in the rule of the vast orbs of heaven, can dispense with the aid of Christians, does He need their help to execute His vengeance in providence?

Does not the fact of vengeance in providence imply that the political or religious pacifist, who would rob the king of the sword, is misinformed of the ways of God, and in thus acting, takes Christian principles outside of the proper Christian sphere?

Does it not also imply that the Christian who acts in judgment is acting below his proper sphere?

But the day is coming in which Christians will have the power of rule and right of judgment. This is stated in 1 Corinthians 6:2. This will be committed to them (according to Rev. 20:4, 5) upon the revelation of Christ to the discomfiture of all His foes, and upon the incarceration of Satan in the abyss (Rev. 19:11; 19:20-20:4).

The Christians of Corinth behaved in a way that amounted to attempting to reign before their time. With some grimness the apostle says, *"I would that ye did reign, that we also might reign with you"* (1 Cor. 4:8). It follows that if rule is not yet delegated to the Church, neither is the power to judge. This is emphasized by the question of 1 Corinthians 5:12-13, *"What have I to do to judge them that are without?"* At present this is only God's matter. He has not yet shared it with the Church.

Hence for a Christian to endeavor to act in judgment is for him to intrude into a realm in which he has no authority yet, to interfere where he has not yet the necessary competence, to act out of order in regard to the purposes of God. By taking that which is the prerogative of God, he dares to rob God (Rom. 12:19).

Even though the exhortations of the New Testament are all designed to withdraw the Christian and the churches from direct intervention in the affairs of the world, there is a sphere in which the believer, and the assemblies of believers, may have a hand in providence as it controls the circumstances of men. A higher realm, spiritual in character, governs the affairs of earth, and it is in this realm that God has been pleased to give believers—both individuals and assemblies—a standing and a power which, by their prayers, they may use for the good of mankind.

This is taught in the New Testament, as we shall see, and exemplified in the Old. The intercession of Moses saved the Jewish nation in his day, even though God had lifted up His hand to destroy that generation of it. (See Ezek. 20:13; Ex. 32:10-14.)

Samuel's power with God brought mercy to a sinning nation at a time when they rejected God and desired a human king; and his life of prayer and faithfulness became an important stepping-stone to the greatest glory of Israel in the reigns of David and Solomon (Ps. 99:6).

The way in which these men are mentioned in Jeremiah 15:1 is evidently intended to emphasize the importance of a spiritual and a hidden ministry of intercession for the circumstances of men. Each stood before God in his day, and by his prayers prevented the calamities that would otherwise have come upon the people.

Elijah too, by prayer, influenced the affairs of nations. We are told that he was a man of like passions as we are (Jas. 5:17), yet he, in his day accomplished by prayer what the combined power of armies and navies could never do.

God does not at any time need the physical help of His people to control His material creation. And though in past or present ages He may providentially move nation against nation for purposes of chastisement, the puny strength of the individual believer or churches is equally unnecessary to help Providence deal with the evils of this age or any part of it. But though in both realms God can well dispense with the physical energies of His people, He desires the expenditure of their spiritual energies in behalf of the spiritual and material good of others. The surprise of Isaiah 59:16 (*"He wondered that there was no intercessor"*) is eloquent support of this principle.

Intercession of this kind is necessary in every age and it will go ill with men if it is lacking. What men like Moses and Samuel did in their day, according to national principles, it is the privilege and responsibility of the churches to do in our day, according to principles which are not limited by national distinctions.

The New Testament churches are viewed dispensationally and locally. Dispensationally and in its widest sense the Church embraces every true believer in the present age, and is called the body of which Christ is the Head

(Eph. 1:22-23). In its local character it is composed of all the believers in any locality who assemble together for specified purposes. Four purposes are clearly mentioned in apostolic teaching: to celebrate the Lord's Supper, to receive ministry, to share in the fellowship of our common life, and to engage in intercession. Several chapters of the Epistle to the Corinthians are devoted to the explanation of the gatherings for the breaking of bread and ministry (see 1 Cor. 11:17 to 14:40), but it is the first Epistle to Timothy that devotes the following portions to the explanation of the objects of a meeting which is vital to the interests of men—the prayer meeting.

The recognition of the way in which Christ and His work are presented, and of the character in which God is portrayed in any New Testament epistle becomes the key to the true import of its teaching. The list[2] included in the ENDNOTES of this chapter reveal at a glance that it is the Saviour character of God which is prominent in First Timothy, and that the paramount object of Christ's coming into the world is presented as that of saving sinners.

Everything that is enjoined on Timothy, either as an individual or for the local church, is with a view to the kingdom which will be unveiled at the appearing of Jesus Christ. He Himself neither took part in nor moved against any of the present kingdoms, but in *"His good confession"* (1 Tim. 6:13) before Pontius Pilate, declared that His kingdom did not belong to the present constitution of this world at all (Jn. 18:36). The charge leveled against Him that His kingship was insurrection against Caesar was patently false.

206

It is also clear that until the dawn of that kingdom, the great object of the existence of churches is to give i) testimony to the Saviour character of God, ii) testimony that the object of the incarnation was to save sinners, and iii) testimony to the fact that the true kingdom is future.

The fact that prior importance is given in this Epistle to the prayer meeting emphasizes that it is an essential part of this testimony—a testimony which is dependent, not on the existence of Christians in the world, but on the gatherings of Christians.[3] It is stated that the breaking of bread meeting has a testimony character,

For as often as ye eat this bread, and drink the cup, ye proclaim the Lord's death till He come (1 Cor. 11:26).

Not less so, and perhaps, as far as the world is concerned, more so, has the prayer meeting a vital place in the present testimony of the churches.

The churches are not permitted the use of physical force, for, said the Saviour to Pilate, *"If My kingdom were of this world, then would My servants fight."* Nor are they instructed to devote any of their influence and power in social or political affairs. So if the prayer meeting is part of the essential reason for the existence of churches by which they manifest the character of God and thus bring blessing to men, and if by that means they can wield a greater power for human good than can the combined force of all the empires, it is incumbent on all Christians at whatever cost to learn the will of God regarding the prayer meeting and then at any cost to fulfill the function of that meeting.

THE INSTRUCTIONS FOR ITS UNIQUE MINISTRY

In view of these facts, a careful considering of the passage which authorizes and explains this meeting is key:

I exhort therefore, first of all, that supplications, prayers, intercessions, thanksgivings, be made for all men; for kings and all that are in high place; that we may lead a tranquil and quiet life in all godliness and gravity. This is good and acceptable in the sight of God our Saviour; who willeth that all men should be saved, and come to the knowledge of the truth. For there is one God, one mediator also between God and men, **Himself** *man, Christ Jesus, who gave Himself a ransom for all; the testimony to be borne in its own times* (1 Tim. 2:1-6).

It is enjoined as a matter of prior importance that in their gatherings Christians shall pray for the circumstances of mankind. It is also intended, as God answers their prayers for others, giving rule and order and peace to men, that Christians shall reap the benefit of being able to live lives of tranquility and quiet instead of passing their days in strained circumstances and and evil times.

The church at Ephesus, and all other local churches too, are encouraged in this passage to take up the ministry of prayer and intercession for men's circumstances. For if God is ready to grant circumstances of good to all, these circumstances make it possible for men to live before Him in some measure of order, and to be saved through the gospel, thus coming to the knowledge of the truth.

That benefits will accrue to believers as their ministry becomes fruitful to others seems to emphasize that the circumstances of men are the object of that ministry. This is similar to the principle of Jeremiah 29:7, in which the Jewish captives were instructed to seek the peace of the city where the Lord had caused them to be carried away captive, and to pray to the Lord for it. It is explained that *"in the peace thereof shall ye have peace."*

In this way the churches of God are to function for mankind as did the tribe of Levi for the nation of Israel. The way in which the Levites were taken out from among the other tribes, and consecrated to stand in priestly service between God and the nation illustrates how the churches are taken out of the nations and consecrated to stand in priestly service between God and the peoples of the world. They present thanksgivings to God for blessings in the circumstances of those who do not themselves thank Him, and offer prayers in behalf of those who do not themselves seek His face.

It is questionable whether anything comes to man, saved or unsaved, apart from prayer. The statement of Ezekiel 36:37, *"I will yet for this be enquired of...to do it for them,"* is probably an abiding principle. Although God delights to give, He also delights to be waited on and it is fitting to His supreme dignity that men seek Him. The Psalmist had this in mind when he said, *"O Thou that hearest prayer, unto Thee shall all flesh come"* (Ps. 65:2).

God will not be without those who stand before Him. In view of the fact that men generally do not, in fact, cannot stand before God, the sacred dignity and privilege of priesthood in their behalf is granted to the churches. This privilege is to be exercised in private as well, but especially in its gatherings for prayer.

Four words are used to denote the nature of the ministry: supplications, prayers, intercessions, and thanksgivings. The difference between the first three words is not easy to explain, but the following suggestions may prove helpful:

• *Supplication* seems to have in view the particular matter of need which we bring before God.

• *Prayers* presents the act of spreading out one's wishes and consequently of the One before whom they are spread out.

• *Intercessions* emphasizes the nearness of communion, giving opportunity to present to God the needs of those not in that state of nearness themselves.

THE SCOPE OF THE MINISTRY

The terms used in the passage to describe the scope of this ministry show that it is to be exercised in relation to all men, kings, and all that are in high place.

(1) *"for all men":* The full force of the words rendered thus in the AV and RV is "in the behalf of, and in regard to all mankind." It is the widest of terms, allowing no limit, nor recognizes any parties of men. Nations as such are not in view. Nor does any kind of men find preference: neither white men nor black men, neither Englishmen nor Frenchmen, neither good men nor bad men; but simply *"for men,"* as His creatures. Irrespective of distinction, God has designed that prayers be offered for all humani-

ty. Just as none are debarred from salvation, so are none to be deprived of the prayers of the churches.

(2) *"for kings"*: Not for *the King* (as in 1 Pet. 2:13, 17), but *"for kings"*; nor is it for good kings but for all kings, whether they are good or bad. Kings affect the lives of so many of God's creatures and because of this are the special object of Satanic influence. Thus there may be an even greater need to pray for bad kings than for good ones, and to ask that the evil which dominates the bad and brings ill to so many might be restrained, while the good that marks other rulers may be retained. Satan and his hosts, by controlling evil kings, can harass the people of God, hinder the spread of the gospel, and make still more harsh the lot of an already groaning creation.

(3) *"for all that are in high place"*: The leaders of men, the pillars of society, civil magistrates and all in whom is vested authority, and whose position is endowed with dignity, are to be served by the churches in the inner courts of the sanctuary of God, because on them much of the structure of ordered society hangs.

THE OBJECTS OF THE MINISTRY

The main object of the intercession of this holy priesthood is order, tranquility and quiet.[4] The purpose of the churches is dependent on their local gatherings. These local gatherings are dependent on circumstances of peace and freedom. And, in turn, peace and freedom are dependent on the prayers of God's gathered intercessors. This is a blessed circle of interdependent things, which Satan would replace with a vicious circle of evil consequences.

211

Disorder, agitation, disturbance and lawlessness render the peaceful, but potent, gatherings of intercessors either impossible or ineffective. And, being either impossible or ineffective, disorder, agitation, disturbance and lawlessness reign without a spiritual ministry to check them.

Lawlessness, that would disintegrate all ordered life and overthrow every divinely instituted relationship, is already secretly at work (2 Thess. 2:7). Unless restrained by a mightier secret power, it will break out in apostasy and produce the great Lawless One, the monster of iniquity (2 Thess. 2:3-8). How great a part the ministry of intercession through the Holy Spirit plays in this restraint we may not now know. It would seem, therefore, that in intercession for the circumstances of mankind, the churches should pray for:

1. the ordered supply of *the means of life,* such as food, raiment, etc.

2. the maintenance of *the relationships of life,* such as marriage, parenthood and home.

3. the support of *the government of life,* such as civil justice and kingly rule.

4. mercy in *the circumstances of life,* such as peace, security and privileges.

As creation with its faithful seasons links hand with Providence in its control of circumstances, it makes possible ordered life in tranquility and quiet. The churches are then to present thanks to the God who thus opens His hand and satisfies the desire of every living thing. The anthems of praise and the incense of prayers are to mingle as they ascend from those who have most fully proved

His grace. Acting on the principle of grace, they minister in behalf of an undeserving and sinful world. They praise Him that the life of its people is prolonged, so that God's saving message may reach men who otherwise might be victims of distraction because of anxiety, and of death because of calamity.

Frequent mention is made of the debt of Christians to the state, but there is an aspect of these things to which reference is rarely made, that of the debt of states to Christians. In the light of this invaluable ministry, it might be asked what is the extent of the debt of states and nations to those who intercede in such a ministry.

FITNESS FOR THE MINISTRY

To fulfill this ministry which is so important to God and to man, the Lord's people will need *"the largeness of heart as the sands of the sea shore"* with which Solomon was graced (1 Ki. 4:29). Those who do not possess this largeness of heart will find in the Scriptures both encouragement and rebuke.

Jonah lived in a dispensation of law, when for a Jew a nationalistic spirit was encouraged by the promises of God. He begrudged mercy to the Ninevites and was saddened at God's magnanimity toward those people. Whereupon God remonstrated with him, and urged the rightness of sparing the wicked Gentile city because of their repentance and the presence of the thousands of children. If it was wrong of Jonah in such nationalistic and legal surroundings to begrudge mercy to the undeserving, it is surely much more wrong of Christians to do so today because they themselves are the recipients of God's greatest grace in a dispensation of grace.

There is a strong affinity between the Epistle to the Ephesians and the Epistles to Timothy. The purpose of the former is to explain the present position of the believer, who is declared to be already enthroned and enriched in the very sphere where the Lord Jesus is seated far above principalities and powers at the right hand of God. It is further declared that the witness and the warfare of the churches belong to that sphere. As the people of God realize the wealth of their spiritual blessings, rejoice in the forgiveness of their sins and their acceptance in Christ, and feel the power of their place with all its dignity of association with their exalted Head, they will find the ability to withstand and surmount, by their testimony and prayers, the stratagems of their adversary the Devil.

While it is redemption and the sacrifice of Christ that give admission to and a standing in the courts of God, there are differences of power on the part of intercessors. The character of those who approach has much to do with the result of their intercession.

In a past age Levi and Phinehas were given the priesthood, not only because they were redeemed, but because of their devotion to the will of God and because they took sides uncompromisingly with God (Deut. 33:8-10; Num. 25:10-13).

Both Abraham and Lot were righteous souls, but only Abraham could intercede for the cities of the plain. He, free of its affairs, treading the genuine pilgrim way, was in the secret of the Lord and could have power with God.

214

But Lot, within the city and involved in its affairs, walking the way of compromise, thus had power with neither God nor man. Abraham, outside, commanded the respect of the world and was powerful in intercession, but Lot, inside, was despised by its citizens (though he sat upon its council), and had no power in testimony to move even his own sons-in-law. Not only was he powerless to bring good to others, he needed a miracle of angelic ministry to extricate him from the judgment. But the intercession of Abraham, although not fruitful in the preservation of Sodom and Gomorrah, resulted in the salvation of Lot from its ruin and consequently the preservation of Zoar as a refuge for him (Gen. 19:29, 17-25).

Moses would never have been the priest that he was had he not refused the pleasures and ambitions of Egypt, and chosen to suffer affliction with the people of God in the pilgrim way.

Samuel's sustained growth in his experience of God developed him so that the noble words, *"God forbid that I should sin against the Lord in ceasing to pray for you"* (1 Sam. 12:23), indicate the sacred value he had learned to set on ministering to the Lord for others.

Daniel, who purposed in his heart that he would not defile himself with the king's meat and who was sanctified even in the midst of an ungodly court, knew the mind of the Lord, and swayed the destiny of nations.[5]

The inspired records of these men indicate to us some of the features required for power with God and show the kind of intercessors who have weight in the courts above.

Surely the groaning of mankind today is a special reason why the churches should rise to this ministry and unite to intercede persistently for the children of men. God delights in mercy even though He brings visitation and will undoubtedly grant that mercy in answer to the prayers which He desires and has authorized.

AN EXAMPLE OF THE MINISTRY

An occasion in Paul's own life provides an example of the working out of these principles. It took place during the voyage to Rome (Acts 27:1–29:10). Unlearned in nautical matters, Paul was divinely guided to give advice. This was set aside owing to the captain's ideas (which were based upon natural wisdom) and the desires of the ship's company for a more commodious harbor. Setting sail according to human desire, they soon found themselves in the very straits of which they had been warned, and were helpless to meet the need of the situation. In the hour of need, the man of God was not found wanting. Conscious of God's purposes for him, he prayed for himself and all the ship's company, and although the lives of all were forfeit, preservation was allowed (Acts 27:24).

The goodness of God in answer to Paul's prayer extended not only the preservation of those who sailed with him, but also resulted in great blessing being brought to the inhabitants of Malta. What influence in the gospel came to the ship's company or to the islanders were are not told, but it is easier to suppose that they were blessed by the gospel as the result of these happenings than that they were not.

During times of providential upheaval the Spirit of God uses circumstances to awaken men and at the same time uses the Lord's people to bear the message of the gospel to those thus exercised. It is also usual to see a time of visitation followed by a harvest of souls.

May the Lord make His people more and more intelligent of His ways in both providence and redemption, so that they may be more effective witnesses for Him in these difficult days, witnesses who can *explain* the ways of God instead of trying to *excuse* Him. And may His people's knowledge of Him and His goodness result in that nearer fellowship with Him, enabling them as intercessors to give more pleasure to Him, and to be of greater blessing to their fellow-travellers to eternity.

ENDNOTES:

1 The Christian teachings of the New Testament strike a higher note than that of normal legal righteousness. A consideration of the remarks, *"Ye have heard that it was said to them of old time,"* and *"But I say unto you,"* repeated five times (Mt. 5:21, 27, 33, 38, 43), will make this evident. It is further exemplified by comparing the statement from the law, *"Thou shalt not steal"* (Ex. 20:15), with *"Let him that stole steal no more: but rather let him labor...that he may have to give"* (Eph. 4:28). The first prohibits the evil of theft, but the second eclipses it, and requires that the converted thief shall labor, not only to be honest, but to become a philanthropist.

Though the Law is thus quoted, and its principles used comparatively to show the much higher standard of Christian conduct, it is not stated that the Law ever properly applies to any other than the Covenant people, the twelve tribes of Israel. Nevertheless, the principles of the Law are found written in hearts (Rom. 2:15) and men are held accountable regarding this knowledge.

2 This list shows the Saviour character of God emphasized:
  a. He is the one who makes all things alive (1 Tim. 6:13).
  b. He preserves all men in life, especially believers (1 Tim. 4:10).
  c. He gives to His creatures all things richly to enjoy (1 Tim. 6:17).
  d. He created all things for their use (1 Tim. 4:3, 4)
  e. He willeth that all should be saved and come to the knowledge of the truth (1 Tim. 2:3-4).
  f. To this end, God in His Saviour character and Christ Jesus, the only hope of those who believe, committed apostleship to Paul that he might be a herald of the gospel of the glory of the blessed God and a teacher of these things (1 Tim. 1:1). This is seen in the following:
  —Christ Jesus came into the world to save sinners (1 Tim. 1:15).
  —Christ Jesus is the only Mediator (1 Tim. 2:5) and Ransom (1 Tim. 2:6).
  —Christ Jesus is our hope (1 Tim. 1:1).

—His Saviour character is also evident in that although He dwells in light unapproachable (1 Tim. 6:16), He has been manifested in flesh (1 Tim. 3:16).

3 What great spiritual importance these gatherings have may be deduced from the following facts:
- —that Satan makes tremendous efforts to frustrate, or divide, or destroy them
- —that flesh always mars them
- —that human arrangements and organizations tend to pervert their character
- —that God uses such exalted terms when He describes them
- —that their influence when properly constituted and functioning brings temporal blessing in circumstances and material things to the world, and eternal blessings of salvation through the gospel to those who believe.

4 The similarity of meaning between the words translated *"quiet and peaceable"* in the AV and *"tranquil and quiet"* in the RV is so close, and their rarity of use such that it is difficult to catch the sense of difference in meaning which is surely existent or the Spirit of God would hardly have used the two, for if the words are identical in meaning, one would have served.

The former word is used only in this passage. It has been suggested that it relates to things without. Strong suggests that it is derived from a term which indicates the idea of lonesomeness, as of being in a wilderness. If this is so, it would appear that the intercession of the churches should be in order that Christians should be left alone to lead lives free from interference, lives, the domain of which should be free from the invasion of untoward and coercive circumstances.

All the associated forms of the latter word, and the uses of these in the New Testament, seem to hold the idea of restrained expression. Its force seems to be directed to that which is within. The use of it (1 Pet. 3:4) in connection with the spirit supports this suggestion.

If these things are so, the ideas seem to be that this ministry of the churches should be in order that believers shall be able to live lives free from outside interference, and therefore free to be altogether devoted to the bondservice of Christ; and unexcited, restrained, self-contained, and quiet as regards that which is within, thus manifest the Spirit of their Lord.

5 The great prayer of the ninth chapter of his prophecy was fulfilled:
   —immediately in that the messenger came with explanation;
   —in a matter of months in that the temple began to be built;
   —in the course of a century in that the city was restored.

His prayer of 2,500 years ago will yet affect the matters of nations at the end this age.

Part Two

CHAPTER SIXTEEN

The Destiny of Nations

The nations formed by God long centuries ago, who have been the subjects of His providences, will, in the persons who compose their remnants, enter into their destiny at the second Advent of Christ. Revealed as King of kings and Lord of lords, He will inaugurate the kingdom prepared in the purposes of God from the foundation of the world. Then the preserved and prepared remnant of each nation will enjoy the blessings that God has in store for men on earth.

God has designed to establish a reign of righteousness and peace under which its healthy inhabitants shall live in an environment as congenial and beautiful as Eden, and as prosperous and wealthy as in the days of Solomon. Nature, liberated from the curse of the Fall, will don a new garment of glory at the command of its Creator King and rejoice to wear its beauty for His praise.

Isaiah rejoiced to tell of a time when:

The wilderness and the solitary place shall be glad; and the desert shall rejoice, and blossom as the rose. It shall blossom abundantly, and rejoice even with joy and singing; the glory of Lebanon shall be given unto it, the excellency of Carmel and Sharon: they shall see the glory of the Lord, and the excellency of our God (Isa. 35:1-2).

The stately glory of Lebanon, the fragrance of Carmel, and the beauty of Sharon contrast strangely with the pollutions of civilization's factories and slums, and the steadier and gentler life of the former with the ruthlessness of modern rush and bustle. Man's lauded inventions, with all their jangle and complexity, will be removed, to make way for God's original peaceful garden scene, and the vaunted excellency of man, in which there are so many paradoxes, will give place to the excellency of God, in which there will be no inconsistency or blot. Luxuriant sunshine and showers of blessing upon delightful nature will cause earth to yield her increase, so that the rich harvest will make the threshing reach to the vintage and the vintage to the sowing time.

In the midst of its wealth and beauty, the animal creation will lose that wildness and lust for blood which have marked it since it lost its due subjection at the fall of Adam. For the lion shall eat straw like the bullock and the wolf and the lamb feed together. A delightful picture of health and safe among the tamed and beautiful animals is given us by the same prophet, who bursts forth:

The wolf also shall dwell with the lamb, and the leopard shall lie down with the kid; and the calf and the young lion and the fatling together; and a little child shall lead them. And the cow and the bear shall feed;

their young ones shall lie down together; and the lion shall eat straw like the ox. And the sucking child shall play on the hole of the asp, and the weaned child shall put his hand on the adder's den. They shall not hurt nor destroy in all My holy mountain; for the earth shall be full of the knowledge of the Lord, as the waters cover the sea (Isa. 11:6-9).

This lovely scene of animal gentleness is enhanced by the mingling pictures of unimpaired and happy childhood. Without mention of years, three ages of child life are suggested: a little child, the toddler of three, four or five years, safe and at home, leads the majestic creatures of God's creation; the weaned child, released from its mother's arms, shall find no hurt will follow its infantile sport; and the child at its mother's breast, so young and defenseless, will need no defense, for no danger will exist even from adder or asp.

These children born to healthy parents will know nothing of sickness and disease: *"Jehovah the Healer"* will be their King.

Then the eyes of the blind shall be opened, and the ears of the deaf shall be unstopped. Then shall the lame man leap as an hart, and the tongue of the dumb will sing (Isa. 35:5-6).

Disease and death which fled before the word of His power when He visited earth in lowly guise, will flee again when He takes the reins of government.

The great variety of national types shall grace the lands

that God has apportioned to them. The mystic character of the Easterner will perceive the deep beauties of the King and the mysteries of His purposes. The relentlessness of the Prussian will be the goad of his devotion to God. The matter-of-fact, the romantic, the demonstrative nations, all will have their place and yield their devotion and homage to the Lord, blending as in the beautiful pattern of a great mosaic. The varied musics and cultures of each land, elevated and restored, will harmonize to praise the Lord in that day.

No armies shall find place in that scene, for they shall beat their swords into plowshares, and their spears into pruning hooks. Returning to pastoral pursuits, they will learn war no more; cultivation rather than destruction will be the tenor of their way and the Lord shall be King over all the earth. *"In that day shall the Lord be one and His name one."*

One supreme absolute Monarch of perfect wisdom and perfect love reigning sacredly as a Priest upon His throne will be the object of the worship of the nations. Desiring to learn His ways, they will seek His temple for instruction. Thus instructed, they will all see eye to eye. And the various nations, with the variety of character in each, shall live in a great religious, social and political harmony, the song of which shall ascend to God from sunrise to sunset.

"A King shall reign in righteousness and princes shall rule in judgment." The Lord, being exalted and dwelling on high, will fill Zion with judgment (discernment) and righteousness. There shall be stability in those times,

abundance of salvation, wisdom and knowledge, and the people shall treasure the fear of the Lord. *"The work of righteousness shall be peace and the effect of righteousness quietness and confidence for ever."* Israel, Egypt, Assyria, Edom, Moab, Ammon, the coasts of the Mediterranean, and all the nations of the far corners of the earth, being ruled in this way, will no more walk in the stubbornness of their own evil hearts, but will rejoice in the knowledge of the Lord.

They will live out their days without deceiver, for Satan will be bound; without contamination, for sin will be swept away; without war, wildness, snare, error, want, sickness, hospitals, prisons, gallows, slums, poverty, oppression, injustice, or ignorance. The sacred wisdom, knowledge, and experience of previous ages, the spread of truth under priestly education, will bless those times.

Knowledge will be diffused throughout the earth by the teachers of Israel and will be inculcated from the Holy Word of God. They will be aided by the ceremonial object-lesson sacrifices in the great Millennial Temple described by Ezekiel (chs. 40–48).

There will be enacted before the eyes of all the nations the great sacrifices of Ezekiel's description. Not that they will put away sin any more than the sacrifices of ancient days did, but they will illustrate the one great sacrifice of Calvary. As the ascending offerings rise before God in fragrance, those born in that age will learn how He, who is their King, once offered Himself without spot to God, how at Calvary He yielded that fragrant life for the glory and pleasure of His God, and as they see the sin-offering they will learn that by His sufferings for them He made purification for sin.

In those days the meaning of Jacob's prophecy will be enjoyed by them all, *"Unto Him shall the gathering of the peoples be,"* and the promise to Abraham will be realized that in Him *"shall all the nations of the earth be blessed."*

He shall be the boast and glory of men, the object of their praise and their fear, and the wonders of His atoning work shall be their sacred meditation. Thus *"the earth shall be filled with the knowledge of the glory of the Lord as the waters cover the sea."*

There is a spiritual direction in human affairs, for *"it is not in man that walketh to direct his own steps"* (Jer. 10:23). We have shown in the chapter on the government of nations that there is a spiritual realm which governs this human realm. At present in that spiritual realm there is a prince of darkness who governs contrary to God and human good. Adam, by his revolt against God, sold himself and his line to the slavery of sin and Satan, who has evolved a system known as the World. So we are told that unsaved men moving along in the ordinary course of life are walking *"according to the Prince of the power of the air."*

But it will not be so in the age to come. The destiny of nations will be a time of emancipation from the intrigues and machinations of the evil one. The day is coming when Satan will be dethroned (Rev. 12:7-9) and bound (Rev. 20:1-3). The places he and his angels have occupied will be filled with redeemed men, whose characters have been molded by the divine education of earthly pilgrimage. Perfected as was their Lord (Lk. 6:40; Heb. 5:8), they will share with Him (2 Tim. 2:12) the rule of the age of regeneration (Mt. 19:28). For *"Unto the angels hath He not put in subjection the world to come, whereof we speak."* At present we see Jesus crowned and God bringing many sons to glory (Heb. 2:8-10), but when that glory shall be fully realized in the unveiling of Christ, men upon earth shall be ruled by glorified men in heaven, headed by that Man who, by the grace of God, tasted death for every man.

Then the human touch, graced by divine character, will administer all the movements of earth. Sinners, saved by grace and perfected to be partakers of His holiness, will graciously administer from the skies a restored earth and an adorned humanity, and will realize for man the destiny of nations and the object of God in the inception and development of nations.

It has often been asked how the great change between the age of the Church and the age of the kingdom in its full manifestation of material blessings will come about. In an endeavor to help along this line, the following section on the end of the age has been penned. It shows that the methods of moral government, which have been partial in the way that they have operated through the ages, will become exhaustive at the end of the age. At the same time they will serve to remove the rebellious of the nations, and prepare a remnant in the midst of each which will enjoy the blessings of the kingdom on earth.

CHAPTER SEVENTEEN

The End of the Age

The Bible unfolds many mysteries of the past and unveils many wonders of the future. We have discovered how God in His providence originated the nations, and distributed them to the lands He had previously formed. We have also seen some of the principles by which their circumstances are controlled. Now our eyes are directed to destinies rather than to origins. Prophecies of future things occupy a large proportion of the Bible. Their object is to enlighten us about the end of this age, to show how it will close and how God will introduce an age of rest and blessing.

Human history has been divided into periods of irregular length, styled in Scripture "ages." The Cross came at the end of certain ages, when Christ appeared to put away sin by the sacrifice of Himself. This crisis of the first Advent concluded a previous age and began the present one, which will end in the crisis of the second Advent at the future unveiling of the Lord Jesus. He will again appear, this time apart from the question of sin, unto salvation (Heb. 9:24-28). This *"appearing of the glory of our great God and Saviour Jesus Christ"* (Titus 2:13) will inaugurate the *"age to come,"* which has been the expectation of inspired prophets, the song of Bible poets, and the desire of the godly of all ages.

The same Jesus who was *"received up in glory"* (1 Tim. 3:16), will come *"in the glory of His Father and His angels"* (Mt. 16:27) and, amidst the myriads of His holy ones, will execute judgment on the ungodly (Jude 14-15). Resurrection will bring to the glory of the new age those who have died in faith; the godly will be recompensed and will enjoy eternal life (Mk. 10:30). The Lord Jesus, reigning in power and righteousness, shall cause creation's groan to cease, liberating it from the bondage of corruption and restoring earth to Eden's fruitfulness and beauty. Nations will learn war no more; a world of redeemed people will unitedly praise and serve the Saviour who bought them and God who blesses them. Then *"Glory to God in the highest and on earth peace among men in whom He is well pleased"* (Lk. 2:14) will be realized to the full.

THE *PAROUSIA* AND TRANSLATION

The happenings related to the return of Christ will require a period of years for their fulfillment as did the happenings of His first coming and His presence among men. This period of years may be as long as those associated with the first coming. Converging on the time of the second coming there are many other prophecies that will be fulfilled at points along its period of years, however many they be. Some have suggested seven, others as many as seventy. There hardly can be fewer than seven or as many as seventy. Perhaps the analogy of the duration of the first coming and what followed in our Lord's presence here will prove to be nearer the truth. This period of years will constitute a transition from the conditions of this age to those of the kingdom in its full glory and is spoken of as the *"end of the age."*

The Lord Jesus is now exalted in the place of highest authorities, angels, and powers having been subjected to Him. As Head over all things, He is seated at the right hand of the Majesty in the heavens, glorified with all the *"glory that He had...before the world was."* What a miracle heaven holds! The glory of eternal deity shining out in His body that still bears the marks of His passion and the anguish of Calvary. At present His power is concentrated on the work of the gospel and the formation of the Church. To this end He acts, as well as in the governmental realm, in the blessed character of a *"Prince and a Saviour."*

Even so, at present the predominating offices He fills are those of High Priest and Advocate of His people and Saviour of all those that in repentance toward God put their trust in Him.

When He comes again, in virtue of the rights won at Calvary, with the full power with which He is invested by the court described in Revelation 4 and 5, He will rid the earth of everything that has not *"Him"* for its foundation and center, and everyone who has not enthroned Him in his heart as Saviour and Lord. His ensuing reign of unveiled and outshining power and glory will be in contrast to the indirect and hidden form of His working during the present age.

In the transitional period of the end of the age, between the present and future forms of His power, the visitations of God that have previously been partial will become exhaustive. Then summary justice will deal absolutely with all forms of sin—political, religious and moral. That generation will bring to a head the sins of the age, and the systems of the present will be displaced by the order more fully described in the chapters on "The Destiny of Nations" and "The End of the Age." The Book of the Revelation, in chapters 4 to 19, deals with both aspects of the same period and shows how Christ will control the providential judgments of God so as to bring the age to the climax of His appearing.

A number of interesting words are used by the Holy Spirit in His teaching of the return of Christ, each of which is a study itself. But it is essential to have right views of the coming to understand the sense of the most frequently used term *parousia*. This Greek word occurs twenty-four times in the New Testament: twice rendered *"presence,"* and twenty-two times given as *"coming."* Liddell and Scott say that it primarily means "a being present." It requires more than the idea of arrival, and emphasizes the consequent presence at the time of, and after, the arrival. Its use in the following places establishes this meaning:

1 Cor. 16:17—the presence of Stephanus, Fortunatus and Achaicus with Paul;
2 Cor. 7:6-7—the presence of Titus with Paul;
Phil. 1:26; 2:12—Paul's presence with the Philippians;
2 Cor. 10:10—Paul's presence with the Corinthians.

It is used of the first coming of Christ when, in 2 Peter 1:16, Peter describes the presence of the Lord Jesus on earth and makes particular mention of His being with them on the Mount of Transfiguration.

Peter uses it again in the third chapter of his second epistle regarding the dissolution of the heavens and earth when the day of God will be present (v. 12).

In the remaining cases, it is used with reference to the second coming of the Lord Jesus. James 5:7-8 and 2 Peter 3:4 use it when speaking of the coming in a general way, but in the following list it conveys four ideas which form a sequence:

1 Thess. 4:15; 2 Thess. 2:1—the idea of meeting His people, who will be caught up to meet Him in the air as the Lord Himself descends from heaven.
1 Thess. 2:19; 3:13; 5:23; 1 Jn. 2:28—the idea of His presence with His people, who have been caught away from earth, and who will be presented before God.
2 Thess. 2:8—the idea of that presence, in glory with His people, shining out to earth to the destruction of the Man of Sin.

At the outshining of His *parousia* (rendered in the Authorized Version, *"brightness of His coming"*), the *"revelation"* of the Epistles converges with Matthew 24, where the disciples ask about the signs of the *parousia* and the end of the age (Mt. 24:3). The further occasions (Mt. 24:27, 37, 39) refer to the same *"brightness of His coming"* as 2 Thessalonians 2:8, and describe the lightning-like brilliance and suddenness of the outshining of His presence to an unsuspecting and sin-blinded world. This results in the wicked being removed from earth as they were by the flood of Noah's day.

TRANSLATION AT THE END OF THE AGE

At present, death is the only way by which men pass out of this world and enter unseen realms. But there are exceptions to the rule: Enoch and Elijah were translated. At the end of the age at least one mass translation will take place, though others may be inferred. *"Enoch was translated, that he should not see death; and was not found, because God had translated him"* (Heb. 11:5). The removal of Enoch in this exceptional way is an illustration of that translation of masses, spoken of by the apostle in his Epistles to the believers at Corinth (addressed at the same time to *"all that call...upon the name of Jesus Christ our Lord "*). He says,

> *Behold, I show you a mystery* (or secret): *we shall not all sleep* (or die), *but we shall all be changed, in a moment, in the twinkling of an eye* (1 Cor. 15:51-52).

When that moment has come, it will be true of all genuine Christians as it was of Enoch, that they shall not be

236

found, because God will have translated them.

The Pauline ministry, which became possible by the gift of the Holy Spirit following the exaltation of Christ (Eph. 4:8-11), unfolds for the first time this great secret. Though the germ of the idea may be discerned in the words of the Lord to the disciples in the upper room,

> *I go to prepare a place for you. And if I go and prepare a place for you I will come again and will receive you unto Myself, that where I am there ye may be also* (Jn. 14:2-4).

Nevertheless, it was left obscure until the teaching from the Throne fulfilled the desire of Christ expressed in the words to the disciples,

> *I have yet many things to say unto you, but ye cannot bear them now. Howbeit when He, the Spirit of truth is come, He will guide you into all truth* (Jn. 16:12-13).

The translation of saints was one of the many things He desired to speak of, which they were unable to receive; but after the coming of the Spirit at Pentecost, truth previously hidden from apostles becomes evident even to young believers.

A knowledge of the times and seasons was impossible to the apostles as they questioned the Lord just before He was taken up (Acts 1:6-7), but less than twenty years afterwards it was unnecessary to write to the Thessalonian converts in explanation of the times and seasons (1 Thess. 5:1). They, although saved so short a time, entered into that which previously was hidden from those who companied with Christ. This progress of doctrine had become real through the continuation of the unfinished teaching by Christ; but when He mounted the Throne He shed forth the Spirit at Pentecost and thus unfolded new revelations explaining the character and purpose of the new age of the Church and the great crisis when

the Lord Himself shall descend from heaven with a shout, with the voice of the archangel, and with the trump of God" (1 Thess. 4:16).

Thus He will inaugurate the *parousia.* It is explained that then the dead in Christ shall rise first and we—referring to believers alive on the earth—shall *"be caught up together with them in the clouds to meet the Lord in the air"* (1 Thess. 4:16-18). In one grand instant, in the twinkling of an eye, the great translation of believers will take place. In a flash they will be changed, as they are winged with lightning-like rapidity to meet Him whom not having seen they love.

This waiting *"for His Son from heaven"* (1 Thess. 1:10) is the proper hope and normal outlook of those who have been turned to God. Out of the commonwealth in the heavens, they look for the Lord Jesus Christ, who shall change their body of humiliation so that it shall be brought into conformity to His body of glory (Phil. 3:20-21). Heaven will be made the richer as the vast Church, gathered out of all nations, having served the purpose of God on earth, will realize the bridal glory for which she was designed and destined from before the foundation of the world. She will then be seen to be *"the fullness of*

Him that filleth all in all" (Eph. 1:22-23).

But the enrichment of heaven will prove to be the impoverishment of earth because of the removal of so many whose presence has acted as salt and light. Hastened corruption and increased darkness will be the result. In the midst of this, God will exert correspondingly greater power to bring to the feet of the Saviour other companies of believers.

For some of the unbelievers who are left on earth at the rapture, however, it will be too late. They will come within the threefold designation of 2 Thessalonians 2:

(1) *"they received not the love of the truth"* (v. 10). This shows that the truth had been offered to them previously, but that they had no desire for truth at all.

(2) *"they believed not the truth"* (v. 12). This implies that they had previously chosen to not believe the truth that was set before them.

(3) *"but rather had pleasure in unrighteousness"* (v. 12). This shows that a choice had been made against the love of the truth that would have saved them, and in favor of their pleasure in unrighteousness.

These unbelievers will not only forfeit the opportunity of salvation after the rapture, but will by their rejection of the gospel ensure for themselves the delusion of the Man of Sin (2 Thess. 2:10-11) and most surely find themselves among the ranks of the apostates who, worshipping Satan's false Christ, will with him go into perdition (2 Thess. 2:11-12). In this way the rapture of the Church will seal the doom of thousands familiar with the gospel.

239

While this is so, it must be made clear that all on earth do not come within that threefold designation. There are millions who have not heard the gospel, for whom God will have a message after the Church is in His presence. As they are free of the condemnation of rejecting the gospel of the grace of God, they will be allowed the opportunity of salvation during the time between the removal of the Church and the dawn of the kingdom. In those days the coming Messiah will be preached throughout the whole world as the Saviour, but with special emphasis on His coming as the King.

This gospel of the kingdom will be heralded to all the nations (Mt. 24:14), the ranks of whom will be swelled by the rising generation who come to maturity in the transitional period on earth. And though their days will be lived in earth's darkest period, the power of God and the preaching of Christ will be fruitful to the extent that a great multitude will be saved out of *"the great tribulation."* They will fill Levitical usefulness and blessing in the sacred courts of the true tabernacle of heaven. There they are seen *"before the throne of God"* through having *"washed their robes...in the blood of the Lamb"* (see Rev. 7:9 to the end).

Omnipotence has servants everywhere, and the sovereignty of God will ensure that He is never left without a witness. Whatever the time or conditions on earth, the *"man of God"* is present and *"vessels...meet for the Master's use"* are found. After the removal of the Church, the company of Revelation 7:1-8, spoken of as servants of our God (v. 3), miraculously sealed, will be raised up for service on earth. They will be empowered by the divine agent of Christ, the Holy Spirit, who will secure the glory of Christ in that day by this ministry of the *maschilim,* as Daniel terms them. Knowing their God, they shall be strong and work, instructing many and turning many to righteousness. Eventually they shall shine as the sun when they in their glory fulfill the type of the Cherethites and Pelethites, who accompanied David as personal attendants, couriers and bodyguard; they will be with the Lamb *"whithersoever He goeth"* and sing that peculiar song of triumph that can be learned by no other (Rev. 14:1-7)

These companies are seen in heaven in their heavenly position waiting for the kingdom age. That they are seen in heaven before the age commences suggests that they are translated from earth as the two witnesses are plainly stated to be (Rev. 11:12). It cannot be that they compose the Church, for they retain their separate Jewish and Gentile character, while those of the Church lose their Jewish or Gentile designation on becoming Christians.

It is well to observe the implication of this, demanding as it does that the economy of the Body of Christ ceased before the tribulation. Those who retain their separate character come out of the great tribulation (Rev. 7:14). If the economy of the body of Christ continued until the great tribulation, then there is no purpose in their being thus separately distinguished. The burden of the Epistle to the Ephesians is to show that all in this age are made one in Christ Jesus. But no flight of imagination could make the 144,000 and the great multitude of Gentiles one; they are two companies in their inception, two companies in their destiny, two companies in their activities in glory. Each forms one of the families of the heavens of which the apostle speaks in Ephesians 3:15 (compare Rom. 9:25-26), sharing with the Church and the sovereign Christ the administrative glory in the coming age.

The magnitude of Christ's work at Calvary is brought home to our hearts as we discern the different companies redeemed in virtue of it. Note the following table:

OLD TESTAMENT COMPANIES

Gentile	*Jewish*
From Abel to the dying thief innumerable millions like Job, Melchizedek, the Queen of Sheba, and the many of whom Christ spoke in the words to the centurion, *"Many shall come from the east and west and shall sit down with Abraham, Isaac and Jacob in the kingdom of heaven"* (Mt. 8:11).	The believing Jews of the whole period from Abraham to Christ. This includes all the nobles of faith and the unmentioned millions who discerned in tabernacle offerings and temple sacrifices the shadow and picture of the nobler work of Calvary, when *"He* (Messiah) *shall make His soul an offering for sin."*

THE NEW TESTAMENT COMPANY

The Church, the *Ekklesia,* called out by the gospel

from all the nations of earth between the day of Pentecost and the moment of the Rapture (Mt. 16:18).

THE GREAT TRIBULATION COMPANIES

Jewish	*Gentile*
The 144,000 Jewish saints who will be the servants of our God in the horrific days of the end (Rev. 7:3-4), miraculously sealed and maintained to do their unique work in earth's darkest day.	The innumerable multitudes saved during the Great Tribulation (Rev. 7:14) from every nation, tribe, people, and tongue, washed in the blood of the Lamb, thus fitted for the heavenly sanctuary and its Levitical work (Rev. 7:9 to end).

THE REMNANT FORMED AFTERWARD

In the section on "The Everlasting Gospel" it is explained that the prophets show God-fearing remnants within each nation, produced by the mercy of God to form the nucleus of the millennial earth. They will be the parents of that vast populace who will praise and serve the Great King in the coming age.

It would be presumption to suggest a number for any of these companies (except perhaps the 144,000, and that number may be symbolic). All these myriads of myriads from every age are saved by the same Saviour on the same principle of grace and the same condition of faith, though they will be brought to different positions in the economy of the kingdom of God.

> *"Christ loved the Church,"* and in His love
> Did for her die, that she above
> Might be the partner of His throne,
> But she is not the fruit alone
> That from the *"Corn of Wheat"* doth grow,
> Which He on Calvary did sow.
> Think of the souls before the flood
> Who trusted in the living God;
> Of Abram and the saints of old
> Who died in faith as we are told;
> Of Israel's thousands who foresaw
> The *End* of all their shadowing law;
> Of nations, tribes, and kindreds who
> Have lived and died and never knew
> Of Revelation's glorious light,
> For whom the Judge will do the right.
> Then, death takes half our race away
> In infancy and childhood's day;
> These, through th' Atoning work are His
> Who said, *"Of such the kingdom is."*
> Then let our minds reach on before,
> Till times of tribulation sore
> Shall overtake the sons of men,
> And see the grace of God e'en then
> In sealing thousands as His own…
> Then think of the millennial bliss,
> When Christ shall reign in righteousness…
> Then, on the merits of His blood,
> He shall the whole creation flood
> With waves of blessing, rich and free,
> For He shall reign from sea to sea.
>
> —from *The Atonement* by William Blaine

244

CHAPTER EIGHTEEN

The Disciples' Question

The disciples who were with the Lord when He turned His back on the Temple, were gripped by His closing words to the Jewish people,

> *Ye shall not see Me henceforth till ye shall say, Blessed is He that cometh in the name of the Lord* (Mt. 23:39).

This drew out the questions, *"What shall be the sign of Thy coming and of the end of the age?"* They desired to know the signs of the end of the age and the great changes that will take place in the transitional period on the eve of His coming as King. He does not disappoint the earnest enquirers, but gives them a word-picture of the generation that will conclude this age, of which Matthew 24:4-34 are a description. Yet even this lengthy account does not content the perfect Prophet and Teacher, who further enlarges and explains His word-picture by seven parables that follow, filling the rest of the chapter and the whole of the next.

The first three parables have special encouragement

for us in our enquiry about the end of the age, and are also the easiest of interpretation, namely, the parable of the fig tree, the days of Noah, and the parable of the householder.

Just as the tender branch and the new leaves of the fig tree are one of nature's signs of coming summer, so there will be signs of the summer of His power and glory when it is near. The point of this parable is to emphasize *the fact of signs,* and to show that the signs of the times and seasons may be read as easily in the moral, religious, and political conditions of the nations as the signs of summer in the leaves and branches of the fig tree.

The second parable demonstrates the *need of signs*; for the days of the end of this age will be as the days of Noah were, strangely animated, distracted and deceiving; the earth dwellers of Noah's day were so occupied that the flood took them by surprise, and, finding them outside the ark of God's provision, swept them all away. There is a need of signs to make the godly in our day aware of the end, and to awaken the unbeliever. For it has well been said that "modern man is staggering between Vanity Fair and Armageddon."

The message of the third parable might be summed up in the words, "forewarned is forearmed," establishing, as it does, *the value of signs*. If the householder could have had a sign of the coming of the thief, he would have been prepared and so have saved himself the loss from having his house broken into. It is clear the Lord wished to teach that there are signs to meet the great need of guidance in the deceptive days of the end, their object being to unmask the evils and untruths. These signs are designed to warn and awaken to prepare for the spiritual and moral dangers of the last days. Here are the most prominent features of the word-picture of the end of the age:

1. wars and rumors of wars
2. racial antagonism
3. unrest among kingdoms
4. famines
5. pestilences
6. earthquakes
7. persecution of the godly
8. installing of the idol (subject of Daniel's prophecy)
9. the greatest tribulation of human history
10. physical disturbances in the sun, moon, and stars
11. sign of the Son of Man
12. His actual appearance in glory

It is not difficult to recognize among these features of the end of the age some of the more severe forms of divine visitation common to previous ages, but evidently intensified and more widespread. They are portrayed symbolically by the four horsemen of the sixth chapter of the Apocalypse, who are given authority over so large an area (one-fourth part) of the earth, with the result that sword, famine, death and beasts of the earth hold destructive sway.

A further feature that we have observed before is found present in these coming happenings, namely a time of intense persecution of the believers who will belong to that period. The earth dwellers vent their rancor on the godly when God rises up in retributive justice.

Most sinister of all, an *"abomination of desolation"* (or, *"that makes desolate"*) standing in a holy place will be the herald of a time of tribulation unequaled by anything that has swept the earth since creation (Mt. 24:21; Mk. 13:19). The Jewish nation will then experience more severe affliction than they have known since the inception of the nation (Dan.12:1). Daniel speaks of a sinister figure who will come to power in the latter days. Paul tells us of one who will even claim divine honors and set himself above every object of worship (2 Thess. 2:4). And the Apocalypse declares that power will be given to him for a short period of forty-two months over peoples, nations, tribes and languages (Rev. 13:5-7). In those days, men will be unable either to buy or sell unless they wear the badge of state homage and emperor worship, and bow the knee to the wonder-working image of the emperor which will be raised up by the False Prophet. He will use his art and cunning on mankind to subjugate them to the great Emperor (see ch. 13 of Revelation).

The extraordinary tribulation and persecution resulting from the presence and power of this person, energized by Satan, will be cut short by tremendous physical disturbances in the heavens and earth. The sun, moon, and certain kinds of stars will be affected; earthquakes will shatter cities and systems; all of which will change earth's face and culminate in the appearance of the Lord Jesus in His glory as the King of kings and Lord of lords.

The storm thus brought to its awful climax will, by

death and destruction, remove the ungodly from palace and cot, and afterward subside into the peace of the thousand years' reign of the Prince of Peace.

In this manner the Lord Jesus described the end of the age and prefaced the description by the words, *"Take heed that no man deceive you."* The idea that the world will improve, its systems get better and better, is a deception. There is no hope for the world. Old Testament prophets, New Testament epistles, the words of the Lord Jesus and the final witness of the Apocalypse unite in one voice, solemnly warning us that to press on in greater efforts to remove the world's troubles will only result in greater troubles. Only those who show *"repentance toward God and faith toward our Lord Jesus Christ"* have any real hope. *"He is our hope,"* and, it is the privilege of every believer to wait for the Son of God from heaven and then watch ensuing demonstration of His power in setting everything right at last.

Whatever the measure of temporal blessing God will grant from our days to the actual end of the age, whatever degree of peace, will be short lived and will be granted more on the principle by which God would have saved Sodom, because of the godly in its midst, than on the principle by which He saved Nineveh, because of general repentance by the people.

The description of the end of the age and its distinguishing signs is not limited to Matthew 24, but is the object of all prophecy. Will it surprise us to find that three-fifths of the Bible is prophecy, and that nine-tenths of the prophetic word converges on the end of this age?

The spirit of the prophets, who each ministered to the needs then present among their own people, is projected into the latter days. So, out of local pictures and nearer happenings, they soar to speak of the end of the age in most of their orations. The anointed eye of the obedient believer and true bondservant may thus discern descriptions of events of the end-time. The prophets saw the burden of Egypt, Babylon and Tyre, depicting things never yet exhaustively fulfilled, even though they appear in some measure to have taken place. They describe for us Israel and Jerusalem, and unfold particulars of commercial greatness, social behavior and political importance that will belong to the nations that surround the cradle of the race in lands at the eastern end of the Mediterranean.

Already current events have brought these lands into prominence, and if we are near enough to the end, a prominence that might well increase. It is not a little unfortunate that the horizon of some students of prophecy has been bounded by certain chapters of Daniel and one or two particular chapters of Ezekiel, and constricted by school opinions. This has affected the whole study and led to predictions that fall to the ground. Had these students given more attention to wider prophetic outlook they would have saved themselves folly, and, what is more, saved prophetic study from being brought into a measure of discredit.

All the Minor Prophets are projected in spirit to the end of the age and all the Major Prophets, too, not to speak of the Psalms and the prophecies found among the words of Jacob, Balaam, Moses and others. There are no signs given throughout the Old Testament to herald the end of the Church age. This is to be expected since the Church itself is a mystery whose truth is not unveiled until the New Testament.

But though there is so much revealed, our short chapter can do no more than touch a few general features that will help us to see the governmental ways of God in the end of this age and the opening of the age to come; we shall therefore, in line with earlier chapters, consider some of the political, religious and moral features of the end, which call forth the judgments which will conclude this age and inaugurate the coming one.

CHAPTER NINETEEN

The Outlook for the Future

THE POLITICAL OUTLOOK

The idea of Federal Rule for earth is becoming current in widening circles. Plans are well on the way for complete European Union and some have mooted a more ambitious scheme for a United States of the World. Statesmen of this and other countries hope that it will prove the solution to many present-day international problems. From a natural point of view it seems the most feasible scheme and the most hopeful way of dealing with aggression and oppression.

Although the idea appears new it has been spoken of before. Tennyson dreamed of a commonwealth of the world and others have visualized a strong imperial league able to control and administer the affairs of the earth. But long before the birth of present-day statesmen and poets, the Bible foretold Federal Rule. In several prophetic visions God has given foreviews of a Great World Union. As early as the days of Daniel the prophet, more than five hundred years before Christ, two visions were given clearly predicting that in the last days, immediately prior to the second Advent, a Federal Empire would hold the reins of world government.

The first vision given to Nebuchadnezzar (Dan. 2:31-45) was of a metal colossus, human in form and composed of gold, silver, brass and iron. The complete human figure was used to depict human rule, from Nebuchadnezzar's time until the days of divine rule in the kingdom of God. The metals denote four forms of rule which have been fulfilled in turn in the Empires of Babylon, Medo-Persia, Greece and Rome.

Just before the kingdom of God displaces all other forms of rule, world empire is portrayed as the feet and toes of the image, composed of iron with an added substance, clay. These two elements are interpreted for us and it is easy to recognize around us now the methods of government depicted by them. In fact their antithesis is the cause of conflict at present.

The iron of the image is a figure of the Roman form of government, the harshness of which is revived in Nazism, Fascism, and Communism which sacrifice the individual to the state. But the clay of the feet, which prevents the full power of the totalitarian element, rendering it brittle, and interpreted as, *"the seed of men"* in the place of rule, clearly sets forth the power of democracy.

Eventually the vision shows a federation of ten kings (Dan. 2:43-44) who jointly administer world affairs. The interpretation is confirmed by the second vision given to Daniel (ch. 7), which by means of four monstrous beasts shows the same succession of empires. The fourth beast is shown with ten horns in its head, which are interpreted as a confederacy of ten rulers (Dan. 7:17, 23-24), who in the subsequent vision of Revelation are said to be united in power and rule for a short time before the heavenly kingdom is realized in the world (Rev. 17:12-14).

It is the purpose of prophecy to show the end, the climax, of any movement with which it deals. Thus the value of prophecy to the Christian is evident, as it shows him how things will turn out at the end of the age. It is made clear in the Book of the Revelation that a federation of the world will not result in peace for the world. As a matter of fact, in spite of all the federation's efforts and power, the end of the age will be a time of unparalleled strife and unrest.

What a world of paradoxes this is! In our days there have been immense efforts for peace, but most disastrous wars. Tremendous energy has been expended and great brains used for the preservation of life and health, but now even more energy expended and greater brains used for the destruction of life. Never was there more refinement in the world, yet never more barbarism; never more education, yet never more blindness; never greater efforts at unity, yet never less cohesion. And in the future, however good the method used or however pure the motives of good men and women, Federal Rule will fail to bring peace, will fail to secure lasting prosperity for men.

Human history is a long story of attempt and failure, more attempt and more failure, greater attempt and greater failure, and it will yet be the story of the greatest attempts, and of their proving the greatest failures—all because men fail to see that circumstances depend on attitude toward God and behavior before Him.

Peace does not depend on condition of rule or order of environment but on the moral and spiritual condition of the nations. Peace and blessing come down from God; they cannot be manufactured synthetically on earth, though the world unite in the attempt. We have proved that the government of circumstances operates according to moral and spiritual principles. So whatever be the efforts of politicians or idealists, the moral and religious evils of the end of the age will bring in their wake all the forms of visitation that human history has seen.

THE RELIGIOUS OUTLOOK

(1) *Present Drift:* The New Testament contains serious warnings about the condition of the churches at the end of the age. A special message is given by the Spirit telling us that in the latter times some shall depart from the faith (1 Tim. 4:1), drawn from pristine truth by other doctrines, taught by no less evil teachers than demons. We are told that these men, hypocritical and having cheated their own consciences, will become the exponents of the teachings that have seduced them (see 1 Tim. 4:1-7). The warning is repeated in Peter's epistle:

There shall be false teachers who will stealthily introduce destructive sects and pursue practices that cause the way of truth to be evil spoken of (see 2 Pet. 2:1-3).

This departure from the original teachings of the Lord

and His chosen followers will be aided by tolerance and lack of conviction on the part of those who do not themselves depart from the faith. A Laodicean lukewarmness and apathy, coupled with lack of appetite for the wholesome Word of God, will rob many of the power to withstand the encroachments of error.

Jude traces the development of religious evil in three stages: the way of Cain, the error of Balaam for hire, and the gainsaying of Korah (Jude 11).

Cain's bloodless sacrifice identifies the way of Cain and makes it easy to recognize in our day those who follow that way. Atonement by blood is the demand of God, satisfied at Calvary by the vicarious death of the Lord Jesus. But those who follow the path of human effort, in contrast to faith in the work of Christ alone, have already started on the path of apostasy. How very largely is this characteristic seen in churches today, as the masses are taught to profess religion, do the best they can, and hope for heaven!

The next stage of evil is seen in the error of Balaam, who was prepared to compromise principle to add to his worldly position and wealth. The true men and women of God in all ages have been marked by readiness to sacrifice position, wealth, and even their lives for the principles they have learned from the Scriptures. But the ranks of those that suppose gain in this world to be godliness increase, and even draw into their number true believers who lack the conviction and faith to stand out against the allurements of the world and the general drift.

The final stage of apostasy is traced in the term, *"the*

gainsaying of Korah." He who was a priest amidst the people of God stood up publicly to oppose the truth. The reader will hardly need the matter to be made clearer. Already in the highest places of almost every religious body in Christendom there are those bold enough to stand up to oppose fundamental truth, teaching what they claim is the way of progress.

The Scriptures hold out no hope whatever of general recovery. In fact, the pictures of the churches at the end are depressing. Even of true believers it is predicted that the time will come when they will not endure sound doctrine, but, having *"itching ears,"* will multiply teachers for the sake of variety of voice and style, and choose them according to the measure in which they please the ear and satisfy the taste of the people. The criterion will not be the Word of God alone, but a measure of the Word of God diluted by, and adjusted to, the ideas of the hearers. No wonder Jude was spurred by a parallel need to exhort the believers to contend earnestly for the faith. But the strategy of the Christian is to build up himself, rather than contend with those who depart from the faith. To this end Jude urges four things upon true believers, so that they shall be able to quit themselves like men:

a. The believer's doctrine: *"building up yourselves upon your most holy faith."*
b. His devotion: *"praying in the Holy Spirit."*
c. The atmosphere of the soul: *"keep yourselves in the love of God."*
d. The outlook and hope of the believer: *"looking for*

the mercy of the Lord Jesus Christ unto eternal life."

Believers who do not continue to build up themselves, and who fail in devotion and hope, will contribute to the decline and aid the tide of religious evil by their own personal defeat.

(2) ***Eventual Apostasy:*** The Book of the Revelation is the book of climaxes, where we find the end of every road. There is a threefold blessing promised to those who will interest themselves in it.

Blessed is he that readeth, and they that hear the words of this prophecy, and keep those things which are written therein (Rev. 1:3).

With this encouragement to read, hear, and obey, we turn to its pages to find the climax of religion and the last picture of the religious world at the end of the age.

The first three chapters are full of instruction, and in them the Lord Jesus is seen judging the churches, condemning evils, commending right, giving counsel, promising rewards, altogether giving us what amounts to a foreview of the *Bema* or Judgment Seat of Christ. At this final assessment of the believer as a servant, some will suffer the loss of the works which have not been pleasing to Him, while others will receive reward for faithfulness.

But it is to the seventeenth chapter that we turn for final instruction. Symbolized by a domineering, rich, unfaithful woman, the religions of the world are united at the end. Instead of their being faithful to an absent Lord, they are described as a woman that is a harlot. No longer poor like her Lord—for His lowly character has been rejected and exchanged for worldly wealth—she has cast off subjection and become subjugating, dominating not only her devotees of all nations, but the throne of world power itself. The picture is so striking that the question starts almost involuntarily, "How did this happen?"

Plans well and deeply laid by Satan, the Prince of earthly religion, and adjusted to the tastes of humankind, will then have ripened fully. This great unity of religious power is the result of a secret system which has operated on earth since soon after the Flood, and has produced every religion of the world in its turn. Those religions, appearing on the surface to be so different, will show under a little examination striking likenesses.

All make salvation largely dependent on human effort, in contrast to the Scriptures, which conclude man under sin, shutting him up to a salvation procured by the death of Christ, so that the glory of salvation shall be to the Lord alone. Justification by faith is the hallmark of the one Truth from Eden to the new heavens and the new earth, in contrast to which justification by human effort is the brand mark of one error presented in many forms from Cain to Antichrist.

It has always been the practice of the evil one to use what is divine and then add something palatable to the truth, just as the woman adds the leaven to the meal, and so corrupts the whole. To preach that man cannot help himself but must cast himself entirely on the mercy of

God, resting only on the sacrifice of Christ, has no attraction for the natural man. But to tell him that he must do his bit towards it and hope that all will be right in the end, flatters his pride and completely deceives him.

To be able to measure anything, a standard is required; and a lowered or adjusted standard will inevitably falsify the measurement. The divine revelation of the Bible is the only standard by which the veracity of religion or the correctness of morals can be measured. If that standard is set aside, deception will be more easily possible. Sin will multiply and increase in seriousness, unheeded and unrealized.

The religions of the world have all introduced into their beliefs and practices things unwarranted by God. By going beyond the Scriptures a large percentage of what is done in the name of God is utterly without divine direction. These fabricated additions have produced a huge human superstructure, hiding the truth, and becomes worthy of the charge with which it is indicted—that of being a harlot. The churches are intended to be stewards of the divine truth of the Scriptures and witnesses to the absent Lord Jesus. *"It is required in stewards that a man be found faithful."* Is it any wonder, then, that the Lord calls an unfaithful religious system a harlot? Plighted to Him, professing His name, she has turned aside to give pleasure to kings of the earth and the men of the world.

Over and over again divine revelations once held in faith and love have been perverted and debased by man. It was so within a century after the Flood. Nimrodism was the product in that day. Again in the days of the

Judges, when idolatry and lawlessness became wide-spread, history repeated itself in the departure of the ten tribes of Israel, in the failure of Judah, in the condition of the returned from the captivity. So it was in the perverted Pharisaism that rejected Christ, putting Him on the Cross. It can be seen in the errors and evils of the third and fourth centuries of the Christian era, in the Papacy and its unmentionable evils of the Dark Ages. Even in post-Reformation days, the same perversion and debasement of truth is to be seen in Protestantism's loss of its "protest," denying today the very truths the Reformers lived and died for.

It may be asked whether there is one religious move-ment today that is altogether faithful to the first principles of truth once held, which the founders of these move-ments bought at so great a price.

In every case the process is the same: introduction of the unwarranted human innovation; development of the social side; the ministry of truth is curtailed; truth is finally replaced with human wisdom, entertainment, and programs. These have served like leaven to corrupt the meal. Like the abnormal growth of the mustard shrub, these influences change the character of the movements to the extent that each has become the resting-place of those who are against God and His truth. It requires only the passage of time and the removal of the true believers from every system for all those systems to come together into the strange confusion satanically forced into union so worthy of the name of Babylon.

The present disunited state of religion is cause for anxiety among many, and efforts to remedy this are in operation. In the end they will attain almost complete success, uniting all the religions of the world in one universal system accommodated to the ideas of each constituent, but meriting, as we might expect, the judgment of God for its unfaithfulness.

Eventually when these religions unite in the coming bed of luxury, ease, and world power, they will find it their death-bed, for the men of the world, banded together in their political federation, will destroy the systems that have duped them for so long, and thus carry out the divine will on what has been so unfaithful to God and His Word, so successful a servant of Satan (Rev. 17:16-17).

MORAL CONDITIONS AT THE END

In a dark paragraph about the last days, the inspired Paul depicts abnormal times when iniquity shall abound and the old evils of heathenism return. He says,

Men shall be lovers of self, lovers of money, boastful, haughty, railers, disobedient to parents, unthankful, unholy, without natural affection, implacable, slanderers, without self-control, fierce, no lovers of good, traitors, headstrong, puffed up, lovers of pleasure rather than lovers of God; holding a form of godliness, but having denied the power thereof (2 Tim. 3:1-5).

This advanced evil in the future has its parallel in the strikingly similar passage of Romans 1, and is produced by the very same means. In that chapter the moral state into which the nations of antiquity descended is described, and the process which brought them into such depravity is traced. The same process is already at work in our day and a foreview of its consequence in general social behavior is given us by the seer of the Revelation.

In ancient days the nations turned from the knowledge of God, rejecting the witness of creation and the light of revelation. Though they professed to be wise, they were guilty of the great folly of turning from the worship of the Creator to the worship of the creature. They debased themselves to the worship of man, birds, beasts and creeping things in turn. The darkening effect of this became evident in deteriorating morals; they became like the degenerate objects they worshiped, and they were debased until their glory was in evil rather than good, and their boasting in the things of which they should have been ashamed.

In our day men have been immeasurably uplifted and enlightened. Directly or indirectly, the benediction of the spread of the gospel, the light of the Bible, and the fear of God have been felt by untold millions in the last few centuries. Wherever the gospel has been received among the nations men have been spiritually, morally, and mentally enlightened. But the old process is already at work, the decline has commenced, the rot set in. Men have been turning away from the light of the Scriptures and the witness of creation into the dim regions of human speculation and reason. Even now some of the old fruits of this refusal to acknowledge God as God are to be seen: selfishness, greed, lack of natural affection, disobedience to parental control, love of pleasure and denial of the controlling power of revealed truth. As time goes on, evil men and seducers from true godliness and right morals will wax worse and worse, deceiving others and being themselves deceived. Professing enlightenment and liberty, they will become darkened in their philosophies and enslaved in their self-pleasing and sin, though claiming to be advancing. For as the true light is rejected, men can only recede into darkness, and a darkness as heathenish and immoral as that of the ancient world.

The conditions of the end of the age will corroborate the saying that history repeats itself. The moral horrors of ancient Rome, the gilded lie of Grecian culture, the superstition and cruelty of Assyrian and Egyptian days, will be repeated, and attest the truth that man is helpless to live aright apart from submission to the Bible, the fear of God, and faith in His promises.

"Higher Criticism" has robbed many of confidence in the Bible, and the hypothesis of evolution has stolen from others the sense of the reality and personality of an Eternal and Almighty God. Giving nothing in their place, these Satanic instruments have laid open many thousands of hearts to the allurements and deceptions of Eastern religions, psychic research, astrology, materialism and a score of supposedly new heresies. Insidiously these things are penetrating the masses of Europe already robbed of the fear of God and faith in the Bible; lawlessness in morals is rampant. To be governed by high principles is now regarded by many as prudishness.

The seer of Revelation describes the end, explaining in

265

a couple of short verses the character and conduct of society when the present leaven has fully worked its corrupting process. A passage from Dr. J. A. Seiss's work on the Apocalypse will furnish us with ample exegesis of the two verses that close the ninth chapter of Revelation:

And the rest of mankind, which were not killed with these plagues repented not of the works of their hands, that they should not worship demons and the idols of gold, and of silver, and of brass, and of stone, and of wood; which can neither see, nor hear, nor walk: and they repented not of their murders, nor of their sorceries, nor of their fornication, nor of their thefts (Rev. 9:20-21).

"Murder will be among the commonest of crimes. Sensual and selfish passion will make sad havoc of human life, with no serious thought about it on the part of the leaders of public sentiment. Feticide, infanticide, homicide and all forms of sin against human life will characterize society, and be tolerated and passed as if no great harm were done. And well would it be for us, if such were not largely the state of things even now.

"Sorceries, impure practices with evil agencies, and particularly with poisonous drugs, is also given as one of the dominant forms of vice and sin in those days. The word specially includes tampering with one's own or another's health, by means of drugs, potions, intoxications, and often with magical arts and incantations, the invocation of spiritual agencies, the putting under influences promotive of sins of impurity both bodily and spiritual. We have only to think of the use of alcoholic stimulants, of opium, of tobacco, of the rage for cosmetics and medicaments to increase love attractions, of resorts to *pharmacopoeia* in connection with sensuality, of the magical agents and treatments alleged to come from the spirit world for the benefit of people in this, of the thousand impositions in the way of medicines and remedial agents, encouraging mankind to recklessness in transgression with the hope of easily repairing the damage of nature's penalties, of the growing prevalence of crime induced by these things, setting loose and stimulating to activity the vilest passions, which are eating out the moral sense of society, for the beginnings of the period when the sixth trumpet is sounded.

"And interlinked with these sorceries, and reacting the one to the other, will also be the general subversion of marriage and its laws, and the deluging of society with the sins of fornication and adultery. The Apostle uses the word *'for-nication'* alone, as embracing all forms of lewdness, but as if to intimate that marriage will then be hardly recognized any more. And already we hear the institution of legal wedlock denounced and condemned as tyrannical, and all rules, but those of affinity and desire, repudiated as unjust. Already in some circles we find the doctrines of 'free love' put forth and defended in the name of right, a better religion, and a higher law. And it would be strange indeed if the revival of the old heathen philosophies and religions, which justified, sanctioned, and sanctified promiscuous concubinage, did not also bring with it a revival of all these old heathen abominations. So also has the holy Apostle written that *'in the last...men shall be...incontinent.'* And here the seer

267

enumerates fornication as one of the outstanding features in the social character of those times.

"And last in the catalogue stands the statement of general and abounding dishonesty, the obliteration of moral distinctions, the disregard of others' rights, and the practice of fraud, theft, and deceit wherever it is possible. Pollock makes his ancient bard of earth tell of a time when:

Blood trod upon the heels of Blood;
Revenge in desperate mood, at midnight met
Revenge; war brayed back to war, deceit deceived
Deceit, lie cheated lie, and treachery undermined
Treachery, and perjury swore back to perjury, and
*   blasphemy*
Arose with hideous blasphemy, and curse
Loud answered curse; and drunkard, stumbling fell
O'er drunkard fallen; and husband met husband
Returning each from others bed defiled;
Thief stole from thief, and robber on the way
Knocked robber down; and lewdness, violence,
And hate, met lewdness, violence, and hate.
And mercy, weary with beseeching, had
Retired behind the sword of justice, red
With ultimate and unrepenting wrath.

"And that time, with just this condition of things, will have come, when this sixth trumpet sounds. We need not wonder, therefore, that it brings a plague of horror and judgment upon mankind, exceeding all that we yet have had to contemplate"[1]

The same road inevitably leads to the same end; and

whoever takes it and at whatever time, will find that every step upon it brings him nearer to the same ultimate destiny. The nations of antiquity trod the road of rejection of God, of the light of the Scriptures and of the promises of Christ. It led them down into the depths of a heathenism which, though it boasted culture, held, too, the grossest immoralities. Modern nations already are advancing along the road of rejection of the personal God, the Creator, and of rejection of the revelations of Scripture and repudiation of the true Christ of the Bible. This same road can only lead to the same end—a modern heathenism, albeit religious and refined, yet holding under that veneer the evils of ancient days.

The same sins, committed by a modern populace, can only result in the same punishments. God will have no other course but to visit upon the sinner of the future the same punishments as He has done upon the sinners of the past. The following argument quoted from another is incontestable:

"We may, a moment or two, compare the state of men at that time with former times, when the longsuffering of God was exhausted, and judgment burst forth.

"1. This day is worse than the times of the flood. Then the earth was corrupt before God, and filled with violence. Here corruption of every kind, both between man and man, and man and the Most High, prevails; and murders, the highest of the crimes of violence, are numerous. Besides this, there are idolatry and demon worship, which are not named as existing before the flood. If then, even in that day,

269

and despite their few advantages, wrath broke out, over-turning the usual course of things, how much more then!

"2. Of the men of Sodom we read *'that they were wicked, and sinners before the Lord exceedingly.'* Sins of Sodom are here, and others super-added. If miracle avenged iniquity then, much more now!

"3. Oppression, rising even to murder, sorcery, and idol-atry, were found in Egypt. But other sins are found here. No marvel then, if plagues like those of Egypt overtake the world then!

"4. Like to these were the sins of the nations of Canaan, when God commanded their extermination by Israel. On them fell supernatural judgments, combined with the sword of the tribes.

"5. The days of Ahab and Jezebel resemble these. Then was there murder of the righteous, and taking of his inheri-tance by fraud; fornication, idolatry, and sorcery. Then fell the judgment of three and a half years' drought. Why should it not fall again on earth under like or greater sins?

"6. These are like the times of Israel and Judah, when Nebuchadnezzar sent and carried them away captive, destroying temple and city. Is it any wonder, then, if the next chapter foretells judgment coming on both the temple and metropolis of Israel once more? The type of the Assyrian came in Zedekiah's days; but now that transgressors are come to the full, the great usurper appears.

"The world has heard the gospel and refused it. Far greater is its responsibility in that day than in any previous one. Far stouter and more deeply rooted is its attitude of resistance than at any former time.

"Things are advancing with no slack pace towards this dismal consummation. Beneath the thin crust of formal Christianity, the germs of these trespassers here and there peep forth. Idolatry is putting forth its feelers; and the giving heed to seducing spirits is already visible. On this basis all the other evils will establish themselves."[2]

ENDNOTES:

1 J. A. Seiss, *The Apocalypse,* (Grand Rapids, MI: Zondervan Publishing House, n.d.), 269.

2 ibid. 438-439. Citing Serp, *The Apocalypse Expounded: Volume 2*

CHAPTER TWENTY

The Process and Climax of Providence

The first nine verses of the last chapter of Zephaniah divide into three portions. They convey in turn: i) the plague of evil in the city (vv. 1-4); ii) the failure of every measure of Providence to correct it (vv. 5-7); and iii) the day when the plague will be stayed (vv. 7-9). Pollution, filth and oppression; disobedience, infidelity and departure from God; cruel princes, plundering judges, light and treacherous prophets, hypocritical priests violating the law they should teach—all describe the moral, political and religious state so deserving of divine visitation.

The righteous Lord without iniquity, not condoning evil, brings daily His judgment to light, seen in Providence cutting off nations, desolating battlements, cities, dwellings and streets. But the hope that the nations will receive correction proves vain: *"the unjust knoweth no shame,"* and even though checked in the midst of visitation, he takes advantage of any respite to hasten again to his old ways of sin.

"Therefore wait ye for me," says the Lord, *"until the day that I rise up to the prey...to pour upon them Mine indignation, even all My fierce anger."* A day is predicted when the judgments of God will be of such a nature as to remedy the evils of earth by removing from it all that offends.

This Great Day of the Lord will be at the time of the *parousia* of Christ, at the end of this age when the trumpets and vials of exhaustive visitation will purge earth of the evils which have from time to time been the reason of His partial and recurring visitations.

The first two sections of this passage give a resumé of the process of God's providence down through the ages, and the third shows the climax of divine government at the end of the age.

The recurring times of visitation and tribulation acting as the flail of Providence, bringing suffering and death to the nations of men, have produced varied effects in different lives. Some are awakened to the knowledge of God and are converted. Others are brought to fear God, but without conversion. Many are hardened, and, in spite of everything, they resist the voice of God. The children of God, never unaffected during the world's troubles, are sanctified and prepared for the kingdom of God.

In times of visitation, the slain are multiplied until, numbering more than thousands, they are counted in millions. As a servant to the godly, Death liberates them from the toil of earth and the bondage of the body, to be *"with Christ."* As a servant of justice, Death removes the sinner from the scene of his sin. The great scythe that mows down the people of earth has a moral effect on those who are spared. The danger, hanging as a pall, sobers men and unmasks as transient all the pleasures and pursuits of sin. But even so, it fails to purify men completely or to recover them from the ways of evil.

At the same time, the cry of the oppressed, the groaning of the prisoner, the hopelessness of correcting others (Jer. 2:30), moves the One *"who will not always chide"* to grant mercy and terminate the days of evil. So God allows the light of morning to follow the night of gloom, the rest of peace after the throes of war, and easier circumstances to come after times of tribulation. So, in His pity and goodness, He again allows mankind to enjoy those mercies of creation and providence withdrawn in days of visitation. The times of tribulation alternate with times of tranquility, wave after wave having their effect upon human sin, but never curing it, salt-like deterring corruption, though never completely arresting it. Salutary for the while, the benefits soon fade in times of peace, when men relax and self-indulgence recurs.

Again and again down the ages and dispensations the waves break and roll back in apparent defeat, until the dread hour arrives when the quick waves of apocalyptic tribulation bring the tide of divine justice to its height. Then tribulation will head up in the *"great tribulation."* Days of the Lord culminate in the *"great day of the Lord,"* expelling the wicked from the earth and sweeping earth clean of every rebel.

It is easily recognized that in modern days the cycles of events are shorter. Everything moves more quickly;

275

tragedies are soon forgotten; salutary effects rapidly fade; impressions made by days of chastening are quickly erased and men hurry back to the very sins for which they and their fathers have been punished. The more rapid return to evil shortens the periods of tranquility, which are followed all the earlier by further visitation.

The accelerated march of events makes all forms of blessing and power short-lived. Sins more seductive become more widespread and, being more widespread, there is less consciousness that what is practiced is sin. In a more general and more popular atmosphere sin develops to greater magnitude. Thus visitations need to be more severe and far-reaching, until those days arrive at the end of the age that are worthy of the solemn designation of the Lord Jesus: the *"days of vengeance"* or *"retributive justice."*

The word translated *"vengeance"* has righteousness as the main idea and of action taken because of righteousness. Justice, satisfaction, punishment are included. The sin of man, the evil of the movements of earth, political, religious, and moral apostasy, will together cause a cry to ascend to heaven which will call forth the judgments of the Day of the Lord.

CHAPTER TWENTY-ONE

The Everlasting Gospel

The end of the age is described in many parts of the Scriptures. Most, if not all of the canonical prophets contribute to the foreview. The Lord Jesus speaks of it as we have seen; Paul, Peter, John, James, and Jude add their quota, and it is left for the last book of the Bible—the keystone of the sacred Scriptures—to give us evidence which will bring all the revelations of the Spirit into line. In the Book of the Revelation the veil between heaven and earth is removed, making it possible for us to see the movements which will take place in heaven at the end of the age, and their reaction on earth at that time.

Ezekiel's vision showed him how the storms of earth in his day were set in motion and controlled by heavenly beings directed by the One who sits on the Throne. In like manner, but in greater scope, the Book of the Revelation shows how the happenings on earth at the end of the age are controlled by ceremonies, prayers and legal contests in the heavens. The triumphant Lion-Lamb who prevailed at the Cross and who has been forming a kingdom of those redeemed by His death, opens in heaven the seals of a momentous scroll. As He does so, powers go forth upon the earth involving war, famine, death, and the persecution of saints, all of which result in the *"Day of the Wrath of the Lamb."*

A careful consideration of the happenings of these seals in the light of other prophecies suggests that a period of years will be required of not less number than the seals. These years lead up to further events on earth resulting from the sounding in heaven of the seven trumpets, and culminate in the awful state of affairs produced among men by the pouring forth of the vials from the Temple above.

It is evident that the apocalyptic judgments take place in three phases—seven seals, seven trumpets, seven vials—each phase accelerating and intensifying the visitations that are so prominent a feature of the latter days. After the six seals have been opened, the seer describes a short, ominous hush. *"There was silence in heaven about the space of half an hour"* (Rev. 8:1), as though Heaven itself is awed to silence at the prospect of the impending storm. Its praises wait; its songs are hushed.

Then the Angel-Priest (surely none less than Christ) approaches the altar to present with incense the prayers of all the saints. Only one kind of prayers by *"all the saints"* is at that time still completely unanswered. (No answered prayers would be again offered at this point; nor could prayers unanswered because they were not according to the will of God.) These are prayers that have been prayed by every true believer of every age, prayers in full accord with the will of God, but which up till this time in the

278

future are yet unanswered. They are the prayers according to this principle: *"Thy kingdom come, Thy will be done in earth as it is in heaven."*

These prayers, expressed by so many, oft repeated, accumulating, though awaiting answer, unforgotten, because kept in the custody of Christ, are now offered, with the incense of His own Person and sacrifice. Thus offered they are swiftly answered. And the answer means that the saints receive the kingdom, the meek inherit the earth, and the mourners and poor in spirit realize the blessings of millennial glory. This requires that the rule of earth be wrestled from the sinful hands which hold it, and that those who are not the followers of Christ be relieved of possession of the earth, so that the true followers of the Crucified, who have waited long, can possess their rightful inheritance.

The unsaved of the end of the age will therefore be removed in the days of the retributive justice of trumpet and vial visitations. God will requite with death every wanton sinner, every flagrant rebel, every pleasure-drunk earth dweller, and all rejectors of God and followers of Antichrist. Operating as did the Flood, of these judgments it will be said, *"One shall be taken and another left"* (Mt. 24:37-40). The sinners will be taken to judgment; earth will be stripped of the proud, the arrogant, the violent, the unrighteous, the defiled, the atheistic and infidel, leaving the denuded nations with only a remnant in their midst.

As there was a pause between the end of the seal visitations and the commencement of the trumpet judgments, so there is a respite before the vial judgments. These vials or bowls complete the wrath of God, and answer the prayers for the kingdom by ridding earth of its rebels. God, who delights in mercy, pauses on the eve of His greatest wrath. The day of vengeance is no pleasure to Him, but a dreadful necessity, demanded by human sin and a rejected salvation. Though He has waited long, He waits again and speeds forth by angelic ministry one last urgent call of simplest character, a message imperative, which cannot be hindered by human means because of its superhuman messenger. It warns of the hour of judgment, urging His creatures to honor God as Creator and Judge, so that all may not be swept away in that hour of the extermination of sinners from earth.

The seer observes,

Another angel flying in the midst of heaven, having the everlasting gospel to preach unto them that dwell on the earth, and to every nation and tribe and tongue and people...

and hears, too, the words of the message,

Fear God and give glory to Him, for the hour of His judgment is come: and worship Him that made heaven and earth and the sea and the fountains of waters (Rev. 14:6-7).

This message, the eternal or everlasting gospel, is a demand to acknowledge God as Creator and Judge and lies at the root of the messages spoken of as the gospel of the kingdom (Mt. 4:23; 24:14) and the gospel of the grace of God (Acts 20:24), but does not contain the fullness of either. While its message is contained in the two other messages, it does not itself contain the further and higher truth of these messages. But, being on the threshold of both, it is intended to prepare the heart for the further revelations of redemption and its blessings.

There is in the recorded words of this message, preached by the angel, no mention of Calvary, no word of forgiveness of sins, no promise of eternal life. Yet it is a gospel, because anything that brings men to a sense of God and the fear of God is good news, though some may not think it pleasant news. Anything that emphasizes to men the creatorship of God is good, because it also emphasizes their responsibility to Him and thus brings a sense of sin, the solemnity of which is emphasized by the fact that God is Judge.

In this way hearts are prepared for hearing the further message of forgiveness of sins through the One who said,

He that heareth My word, and believeth on Him that sent Me, hath everlasting life, and shall not come into judgment... (Jn. 5:24).

It seems unreasonable to suppose that men will show repentance toward God, unless they are made profoundly conscious of God and of their responsibility to Him their Creator and their Judge.

This recalls a point established in the chapter on "The Objects of Divine Visitation," where we saw that it was designed that Providence should bring the indifferent, the atheistic, infidels and the materialistic to confession of the existence and power of God. Charles Finney, in his *Lectures on Revival*, draws attention to this principle, that the happenings of Providence awaken men and women, and prepare the way, thus contributing to the work of salvation through the message of Christ. It was so with the Philippian jailer who was awakened by the earthquake, and through it and the succession of circumstances was made to cry, *"What must I do to be saved?"* (Acts 16:30). The ready reply of the apostles presented the Lord Jesus Christ as the object of his faith, and, as they went on to speak the Word of the Lord to him, the result was the conversion and baptism of the erstwhile hardened sinner.

There is a great need of a message like this to awaken men in our day when so many deny the Creator character of God. But there will be a much greater need in the days of the advanced evil of the end of the age. Men have strange success in shutting God out of their thoughts and an uncanny aptitude at turning to themselves for solution to their problems. They begrudge the honor due to Him who made them, and refuse to fear Him who holds them responsible.

God who has borne long with an unbelieving and wicked world, to which He sent His Son and to which—for twenty centuries—He has heralded the great message of His grace. At length, at the end of the age, the long-suffering of God comes to an end. Yet so that some may escape the exterminating judgments, an imperative word hastily goes forth. The alternatives are clear, the issues plain: homage or judgment. Men must then give God His due homage as their Creator and fear as their Judge, or be removed from the earth, which is doubly His, both by right of creation and of redemption.

It seems that the everlasting gospel, belonging as it does to the realm of Providence, results only in physical preservation from the destruction of the last plagues. Those who do not heed its message will be taken, whereas those who obey will be left on earth. As in the days of Noah, when the flood took away the ungodly, leaving the remnant in the ark to emerge into another age, so those who at the end give heed to the message then proclaimed will be preserved from the destruction of the last plagues, and thus will be found on earth at the appearing of Christ in glory. But though thus preserved, the vision of Christ is required for their salvation. They seem to be those of all the tribes of the earth who will wail because of Him (Rev. 1:7), and among whom will be found the sheep spoken of in Matthew 25.

With the remnant of Israel, these remnants of all the nations will join in the contrition and confession of Isaiah's passion song:

For He shall grow up before Him as a tender plant, and as a root out of a dry ground: He hath no form nor comeliness; and when we shall see Him, there is no beauty that we should desire Him. He is despised, and rejected of men; a man of sorrows and acquainted with grief: and as one from whom men hide their face He was despised, and we esteemed Him not.
Surely He hath borne our griefs, and carried our sorrows; yet we did esteem Him stricken, smitten of God

and afflicted. But He was wounded for our transgressions, He was bruised for our iniquities; the chastisement of our peace was upon Him; and with His stripes we are healed. All we like sheep have gone astray; we have turned every one to his own way; and the Lord hath laid on Him the iniquity of us all.

He was oppressed, and He was afflicted, yet He humbled Himself and opened not His mouth; He is brought as a lamb that is led to the slaughter, and as a sheep before her shearers is dumb; yea, He opened not His mouth (Isa. 53:2-7).

As the Spirit of God shall be poured upon these of all flesh, they will see—in His rejection and death on the Cross—God's incomparable grace at the hour of man's greatest crime. They will perceive that the Lord Jesus became the sacrifice for their sins, and realize that His atoning work meets their need as well as the need of the unnumbered millions of believers of every age. Those who compose the remnant of each nation will at the throne of His glory be declared to be the sheep, the righteous. Possessing everlasting life, they will enjoy the kingdom prepared and realized at last (Mt. 25:31 to end).

OLD TESTAMENT EVIDENCE OF THE REMNANTS

Two prophecies, to be fulfilled at the end of the age, give a detailed account of the preservation of remnants in the midst of nations. This occurs when all the nations come under the visitations of the great day of the Lord.

Zephaniah's third chapter tells of a remnant of Israel, and Isaiah's nineteenth chapter of a remnant of Egypt. It is required that other nations be in the millennium, as our chapter on the destiny of nations shows. The way God will bring a remnant of these two nations through into the blessings of the Kingdom Age illustrates how He will, at the same time, bring remnants of all those nations through the storms of judgment. Each passage shows that God will humble the pride of each nation and judge the particular form of it expressed in each tribe. By means of these remnants He will fulfill the purposes spoken of in Acts 15:16-18,

> *...rebuilding the tabernacle of David...the residue of men seek after the Lord and all the nations upon whom My name is called.*

AN EGYPTIAN REMNANT

The story of Egypt at the end of the age shows its leaders self-sufficient, evolving their policies regardless of God, and the nation religiously given to idolatry, necromancy, spiritism and soothsaying, guilty of political and moral pride. She is reduced by the failure of the Nile. This causes the ruin of fisheries, agriculture, and manufacturing and consequently the discomfiture of the princes and counselors, and the breakdown of the morale of the people. The collapsing state thus becomes an easy prey to an enemy and is subjugated by a cruel lord. By restricting the flow of the river on which they depend, God reduces the independent and proud state to a condition of vassalage to another. The oppression following causes many in their misery to cry to God:

For they shall cry unto Jehovah because of the oppressors, and He will send them a saviour and a defender and He shall deliver them. And the Lord shall be known unto Egypt and the Egyptians shall know the Lord in that day; yea, they shall worship with sacrifice and oblation and shall vow a vow unto the Lord and shall perform it. And the Lord shall smite Egypt, smiting and healing; and they shall return unto the Lord and He shall be intreated of them, and shall heal them...In that day shall Israel be third with Egypt and with Assyria a blessing in the midst of the earth: for that the Lord of hosts hath blessed them saying, Blessed be Egypt My people, and Assyria the work of My hands, and Israel Mine inheritance (Isa. 19:20-25).

So by reducing the proud, destroying the arrogant and antagonistic, removing the evil by the sword, famine, pestilence, and miraculous earthquakes and judgments of the Apocalypse, God will produce a suppliant nucleus among those that remain, a remnant calling on His name from whom He will repeople the millennial earth.

A JEWISH REMNANT

In like manner the Jewish nation shall righteously be brought into the most intense fires of all their history, *"the time of Jacob's trouble,* which will prove to be for that nation:

...a time of trouble, such as never was since there was

a nation even to that same time: and at that time thy people shall be delivered, every one that shall be found written in the book (Dan. 12:1).

By means of these severe providential dealings, God will take away out of the midst of Israel those that are proud, and they shall no more be

...haughty in My holy mountain. But I will leave in the midst of thee an afflicted and poor people, and they shall trust in the name of the Lord (Zeph. 3:11-12).

In the end-days *"the many"* of Judah will be regathered to their land and the *"children of the violent among thy people shall lift themselves up to establish the vision; but they shall fall"* (Dan. 11:14). Great attempts will be made by nationalistic Jews in a spirit of self-sufficiency to realize for themselves the promised blessings upon their nation and land. Looking to themselves and to others for help rather than to God, they will endeavor to reinstate themselves.

Having gained riches and developed the land long barren, they will covenant with other powers for protection; and, rebuilding their temple, they will restore the ancient rites and rest upon earthly princes for military protection. But their covenant will prove as a *"bed too short to lie outstretched upon, and whose covering will be too narrow to wrap in"* (Isa. 28:20). For the Lord will rise up in visitation, and their merchandise and riches will evaporate; the covenants produced by scheming and intrigue will treacherously be broken, and, cheated of the promised protection, they will be the victims of the malice of every nation. Into such a *"wilderness of the nations"* will God allow them to be brought (Ezek. 20:35). Purging out the rebels, He will bring forth the purified remnant and take His abode among them again.

To the afflicted and waiting remnant of Israel will the Lord Jesus be revealed and they, looking on Him whom they pierced, shall mourn, every family apart, rich and poor, priestly and royal, mourning as for an only son (Zech. 12:10–13:3).

The remnant of Israel shall not do iniquity, nor speak lies; neither shall a deceitful tongue be found in their mouth: for they shall feed and lie down, and none shall make them afraid (Zeph. 3:13).

The comforting word of the King will they hear at last:

Sing, O daughter of Zion; shout, O Israel; be glad and rejoice with all the heart, O daughter of Jerusalem. The Lord hath taken away thy judgments, He hath cast out thy enemy: the King of Israel, even the Lord, is in the midst of thee: thou shalt not see evil any more.
The Lord thy God in the midst of thee is mighty; He will save: He will rejoice over thee with joy, He will rest in His love, He will joy over thee with singing.

So, smiting and healing, purging and refining, will God have for Himself a remnant of every nation called by His name and Israel in the midst of them—contrite and dependent, in thankfulness and praise ready to do the will of God on earth, as that will is done in heaven.

Scripture Index